MUHAMMAD ALI
AND ME

by Jean Dancy

Muhammad Ali
and Me

by Jean Dancy

Published by InHouse Publishing

Printed in the United States of America.

Cover concept: Jean Dancy and Ava Monroe

Editor and project manager: Ava Monroe

Except where otherwise credited, photographs appearing in this book are from the personal collection of Jean Dancy.

ISBN: 978-0-9702779-4-7 (Hardcover)
ISBN: 978-0-9702779-7-8 (Paperback)

Library of Congress Control Number: 2018947806

ISBN: 978-0-9702779-0-9 (e-Book)

InHouse Publishing
Inhousepublishinginfo@gmail.com

To reach Jean Dancy:
www.JeanDancy.com
Twitter: JeanDancy8
Instagram: Jean Dancy

This book is dedicated

to my precious mother,

Katie…

who taught me that

ALL of my dreams could

come true…

and she was right.

Acknowledgments

God, I thank You for allowing me to meet Muhammad Ali, for allowing me to take this journey, and for giving me the strength and wisdom to do it well. I have no regrets. When boxing decisions were far too overwhelming for me and I needed to know what to do, I called You. God, thank You for answering every time I reached out for You. You were never on vacation. The line was never busy and I never reached an answering machine. Your loving kindness *really is better than life*...and my lips will forever praise You. *(Psalm 63:3, KJV)*

Marty, thank you for seeing the diamonds hidden inside of me and causing them to shine, for breathing love into my heart and making it sing. Thank you for loving me *exactly* the way I wanted to be loved; for always making me feel loved, appreciated, and so adored...for being my partner, my best friend, my king...and my precious husband. And I could thank you for at least a million more things that only God can whisper in your ear. Thank you!!!

Ava, I would still be carrying this book in a baby carriage without your help. I thank God for you. You amaze me. I see a different shade of your brilliance every day. I have seen you take this book from the baby carriage to college.

You have been quite the drill sergeant though. We worked all night when we felt like it and we worked all night when we did *not* feel like it in order to meet your deadlines. I grew accustomed to seeing daylight before I went to bed.

I have the highest admiration for you as a businesswoman, but I admire you most as a woman of God. Thank you...thank you... thank you!

Saying, "Thank you," a million times wouldn't be nearly enough times for what you've done in my life. Ava, sometimes you were taking me too fast; and I had to run to catch up with you. You were never shy about making executive decisions. You are an extraordinary editor, although you pinched my toes at times. You are my baby, my blessing, my best friend...and I adore you.

This book is written from my very vivid recollections of events that happened in my life, along with help from my journals. All dialogue came from handwritten accounts rather than from tape recordings.

The events in this book are true. They actually happened. Although some of the names have been changed to protect the privacy of individuals, the characters are real.

I have presented the true characters as they presented themselves to me. All of the events in this book have been shared sincerely.

Contents

Introduction

MUHAMMAD ALI IS easily one of the greatest men who ever walked planet Earth. No person in the universe has ever been more captivating, charismatic, or exciting.

No star in the galaxy has ever been brighter than Muhammad Ali.

The world doesn't have a measuring device that can accurately calculate Ali's impact on humanity.

Ali was so much more than a boxer. He was a poet, a speaker, a philanthropist, a philosopher, a global citizen, Civil Rights Activist, Human Rights Activist, Women's Rights Activist…and so much more.

No other boxer has ever left the ring—for over three years—in his or her prime, returned to the ring, **dominated** the sport, and captured the world's attention and adulation as he has.

I will forever be grateful to God for allowing me to meet Ali, get to know him, and call him my friend. It's an *honor* for me to share precious memories about him with you.

Muhammad Ali stands alone—

among boxers, among men—

among people.

Preface

THERE IS NO bigger name or icon on planet Earth than Muhammad Ali (among mere human beings); and despite the odds, God allowed my footsteps to meet at the *same* place…and at the *same* time…with *his* footsteps.

My biggest dream—in life—was to meet Ali, but God had something far greater in mind.

This is the story of a little girl who wanted to meet Muhammad Ali… the lengths she took on that journey…and what happened when her dream finally came true.

Faith doesn't have a calendar or a clock.

— Jean Dancy

ONE

Mother Knows Best

AS HE WALKED through the door, he seemed at *least* 10 feet tall!!! And he seemed to have famous spray all over him. Clearly, he was larger than life to me. Seeing him was too much to take in and process at one time. I felt like there was some kind of short circuit going on inside of me. I was breathing more rapidly than ever before, crying, and trying to stand up. I didn't know how much longer I could stand. For a moment I felt like a balloon and the helium was about to take me up…up…and awaaay!

I was holding on to the Information booth for dear life! The closer he came to me, the weaker I became. And although my heart was saying, "Yes, yes, my dream has finally come true;" I heard my mouth saying, "No…no," as he reached me…and extended his hand toward my left shoulder.

It all started when I glanced the TV one day…and became hypnotized and totally mesmerized by a man's words. That moment changed the entire trajectory of my life.

I was just a little girl, not even a teenager yet. As I was leaving the living-room, I heard an exciting, charismatic voice on television that caused me to stop in my tracks. Muhammad Ali was saying what was going to happen to his opponent in Ali's upcoming fight. He was totally captivating and invigorating and his words kept swirling around in my head.

Me: Momma, I *have* to meet him! Please let me know if you hear what happened in the fight.

Momma: Okay, darling…I'll let you know.

As fate would have it, a few days later I was standing in the same spot when Ali was on TV talking about what he had done in the fight. His prediction had come true!

Me: Momma, I've got to meet him! I have to talk with him about this!

Momma: You *will* meet him, sweetie; and you'll get to talk with him about this and about anything else.

Me: (So excited) Momma, I want to have dinner at his house! Do you think I can have dinner at his house?!

Momma: Nothing is too hard for God. It's just as easy for God to let you have dinner at his house…as it is for God to allow you to meet him.

Me: Momma, I've already been praying for him…since I first saw him on TV.

Momma: That's good! Cover him in your prayers. And there's one other thing…when you ask God to do something for you—your job is to *believe* that God will do it.

Me: Momma, I believe that I will meet Muhammad Ali and I will have dinner at his house!

Momma: Now that you *believe* it, God will take care of the rest… the details!

From that moment on, it was in cement for me. I didn't have any doubt at all. In fact, I started telling anyone who would listen that I was going to meet Muhammad Ali.

Daddy thought it was the cutest thing ever that I was interested in boxing. Me…a little girl…interested in boxing!

I wrote papers about him in school. I argued with anyone who talked against him. And I felt that he had become a part of me.

When I argued about him, as if we lived in the same house, people wondered how I could get so upset. People would say, "You don't even know him!" I felt that I knew him though…on some level.

I believed that there was a little chip inside of him and a little chip inside of me; and I believed those little chips would be activated when he and I first saw each other. Okay…okay, maybe not little chips, but

I believed that he would be drawn to me. That he would want to meet me too. Seriously.

People used to ask me why he would want to meet me too. I felt that he would recognize—immediately—that we were the same kind of people. In much the same way that identical twins who had been separated at birth would recognize each other. I loved him so much! And I thought of him often—the way I'd think of a precious big brother.

As time went on I prayed for his wife and children. I prayed for his marriage. I wanted him to have a wonderful, happy marriage. I prayed that he would win all of his fights and I asked God to protect him in those fights.

I spent so much time daydreaming about that day—the actual day that we would meet. I always saw him seeing me…and walking over to me. I never saw myself approaching him. Though I would have. I certainly had the nerve to do so. I wasn't the least bit shy. I had conversations with Ali all the time—in my mind and in my journals. Sometimes, and don't laugh, I would actually talk out loud to Ali! I would ask him questions and try to imagine his answers. Then I would say to *myself*, 'I can't wait to share this with Muhammad.'

My dream is louder than anything you could ever say.

— Jean Dancy

TWO

Faith Sees Anyway

MY ELEVENTH GRADE teacher (a slim, blonde woman, about sixty years old), had given us an assignment. In her slow southern drawl, she said, "Class, write an essay about what you will have done ten years from now."

After the papers had been written and she returned them, she asked me to stand. Her words felt like bullets as she tried to destroy my dream of meeting Muhammad Ali. She said Muhammad Ali was a global icon and that millions and millions of people all over the world wanted to meet him. Winning the lottery was far more likely to happen in her opinion.

Teacher: Dancy, thinking that you will evVER meet Muhammad Aleee is what is called (and she hit the word *called* like she was hitting a bass drum) an un-REAL Listic expectaaation! It *can't* happen! It just *can't*. Do you think Muhammad Aleee is coming to Alabama?

Me: I've never thought about where we would meet.

Teacher: I could see it better if you were in New York or somewhere like that. Don't you think he'll have security? And how do you plan to get past them?

Me: I've never thought about that.

Teacher: Okay Dancy, let's just saaay that you actually get to see Muhammad Aleee in New York or some place like that. And let's just saaay you got past his security. And let's just saaay you actually got to shake his hand. I'll give you that. That could actually happen. It's one in a million...but it could happen. But HOW do you plan to have DinNer at that man's HOUSE?!! Now, that caaan't happen. It just caaan't!!!

Me: I don't know where I will meet Muhammad Ali. And I don't know how we will meet. But we WILL meet. And I WILL have dinner at his house. You'll see. I wonder what we will eat!

The students laughed and loved the fact that I didn't back down from my dream. Her statements didn't bother me at all. Not even a little bit. I was wearing a "bullet-proof" vest on the matter. Anyway, it was impossible to have *my* mother and be adversely affected by what others said or thought. My older sister, Bonnie, and I were fed a steady diet of love and faith every day at home.

My mother was a brilliant, beautiful woman of God...a career student, only moments away from finishing her Ph.D. in Education. However, she refused to leave the classroom. Momma said all of the magic happens in the classroom.

Momma was an amazing, gifted teacher, known for her kindness and her ability to motivate students. Momma had given wings to so many of her students' dreams. She poured the same love and kindness on her students that she poured on us. Therefore, she could not understand how a teacher, *any* teacher could try to put a damper on someone's dream.

I love writing and I was so excited about the assignment. Everybody knew I'd be writing about Muhammad Ali. She tried to destroy my dream of meeting him. However, the assignment made me even *more* excited about meeting him.

Love is being there…anyway.

— Jean Dancy

THREE

Ali vs. Frazier

MUHAMMAD ALI SIGNED a contract to fight Joe Frazier…
and that put so much pressure on me. People were talking about
it everywhere. Some people said that Joe Frazier would shut Ali's
mouth and bring him down from his high horse.

I had so many concerns for Ali, like a mother sending her child off
to preschool. I didn't want Ali hurt, I didn't want him to lose the
fight, and I didn't want his ego bruised. I wanted him to stay on his
high horse.

I was particularly concerned about his ability or inability to handle
a loss…if…I didn't even want to think about that. Though I had
become a teenager, my love for Muhammad Ali was the same. No,
it was even greater.

None of my friends were interested in boxing but my best friend, Sandra, agreed to go with me to see the fight in a theater.

Before the fight started it was a wild scene. People were hyped like they were on helium. I sat quietly in my seat praying for Muhammad. I could see that the fight didn't mean the same thing to them as it meant to me.

When I heard people saying negative things about Ali, a part of me wanted to lash out at them with my tongue…as only I could do. Oh trust me, I could have shut them all down immediately. I had a reputation for winning all verbal battles. But I decided to put ALL of my energy into praying for Ali.

Every round of the fight was torture for me because I needed to know exactly how Ali was feeling. It was not fun for me to watch because every time Joe hit Muhammad, I felt like Joe was hitting me too! Even when Muhammad was floating like a butterfly and stinging like a bee, I was concerned about how Joe would retaliate. When the fight was over, I felt like a big balloon that someone had stuck with a pin—and let all of the air out of it. I was almost too drained to hear the decision. And then…the unthinkable happened. They gave the decision to Joe Frazier!

With all of the noise and commotion going on around me, my head was down. I wrapped my arms around myself, and rocking back and forth, I cried and cried…and cried. Not a silent little cry either. People could hear me and I didn't care.

Sandra: JeanDancy (she always ran my name together), do you plan to sit here and cry forever? We have to go home you know.

Me: I just need to know how he's doing! I will *never* turn my back against him. No matter WHAT! I'm not that kind of friend.

Sandra: FRIEND?! Let's get a grip here. You do NOT. KNOW. THAT. MAN. JeanDancy! I don't understand how you can get yourself this worked up over a fight...over a man that you don't even know. A man that you have *NEVER* met!

That was a sad night for me. And I was almost holding my breath until I saw him on TV again. I desperately needed to know how he was doing. When I got home, Momma gave me so much love and hugs and comfort. She always made everything better.

However, Ali handled the situation far better than I thought he would. I had even more love and admiration for him after the decision wasn't given to him.

He was my gallant hero. He had shown the world that he could handle adversity and accolades with equal aplomb. The crown on his head was still there and in my mind, it was an even bigger crown.

I was 100% loyal to Muhammad Ali. But in truth, I was totally loyal to all of my friends...to all of the people that I loved.

I will not count myself out...before the winner is announced.

— Jean Dancy

FOUR

New York, New York

THE SUMMER AFTER I finished high-school I went to New York. My best friend and her sister, LaVerne, were there. I remember walking in front of the NBC building and getting a huge revelation. I said, "I have to work here because this is where I could meet Muhammad Ali! This is where they tape The Tonight Show."

The friends who were with me that day didn't want to go inside because they didn't feel that any of us could get a job at NBC.

Friend: Why would NBC hire you?

Me: I can't see why NBC wouldn't hire me. I will get a job there. I have to.

I couldn't wait. I went in the same day and asked if they were hiring. As fate would have it, they were actually hiring.

There I sat in NBC Studios. I took a deep breath and looked around and all of the young ladies (six others) who were seeking the position had blonde hair and blue eyes. Not literally. But none of them were Black.

The interview consisted of several parts. A typing test, a written test, and the actual face-to-face interview. We (the applicants) were all in the same typing room. I looked over to my left and to my right at the other ladies and their fingers were moving faster than the speed of light; and they weren't even looking at their keyboards. I still felt like Superwoman as I pecked each word out carefully. In the end, the lady administering the test said that I had gotten the lowest typing score she had ever seen. I typed 33 words per minute and many of those were wrong.

However, being the only Black woman there with the lowest typing score didn't deter me at all. Not one bit. I realized then that I would have to rely on the written test (that I knew I'd ace) and the face-to-face interview to save me. If I could do nothing else, I could talk. That was my gift from God.

As we lined up for the face-to-face interview, I made sure that I was last. Each of the other applicants went in for about 5 minutes or less. Alas, it was my turn. During the interview at NBC, Al (the head of Guest Relations) and I laughed and talked for over 20 minutes.

Al: You are very articulate and very delightful. Not shy at all. Just the kind of person we want for this position. We can always get somebody else to help with the typing. You could walk out here and see Sammy Davis Jr., Frank Sinatra, the Supremes…anybody. The biggest celebrities in the world are here. Are you comfortable with that?

Me: Celebrities don't intimidate me at all. That's not a problem. However Al, I'm going to be honest with you. If I EVER look up and see Muhammad Ali, I have no idea what I will do! Only God knows what I will do.

In what had seemed like an almost supernatural feat, you guessed it! I GOT THE JOB! A week later, I had a job organizing audiences for THE TONIGHT SHOW! I was in charge of all the tickets that the general public received.

People from all over the world offered me watches, money, and all sorts of things. They wanted to get into the show on a certain night to see Johnny Carson and his celebrity guests. I turned everything down. There was no way that I was going to do any of those things or jeopardize my chance to meet Muhammad Ali there.

Every dream has an address.

— Jean Dancy

FIVE

NBC

ALL OF MY co-workers and their cousins at NBC knew that my biggest dream—in life—was to meet Muhammad Ali. I had everybody on the lookout for him. From time to time, no, actually quite often, the people who I worked with would play a joke on me. It was the same joke every time. And they got the same results every time.

Jennifer: Guess who's going to be on The Tonight Show tonight?

Me: Who?

Jennifer: Muhammad Ali!

Me: (Breathing rapidly, after having fallen against a wall) Oh my… Oh my goodness! What am I going to do?!!! Oh…Oh…I don't know if I'm ready!

Everybody in the lounge would laugh themselves almost to tears. Then someone would tell me it was just a joke. Another equally effective version went like this…I'd walk in and hear these words:

Beth: Jean Dancy probably already knows that Muhammad Ali is on The Tonight Show tonight.

Me: (Breathing rapidly. Falling on the couch or nearest stable object and even sometimes falling on random people.) WHAAAAT?!!! OH…OH…I have to get myself together. Oh my gosh! My day has FINALLY come!

They would laugh so hard! I was more dependable than the mail man. They would tell the same joke and I would give them the same show with all of the same drama. For some unexplainable reason, maybe just being spurred on by my desire for it to be true, I believed it—wholeheartedly. Every. Single. Time. I wasn't even angry with them after finding out it wasn't true. Those few moments of unbridled hope and joy were worth it all…every time.

One day as I was entering the building, I decided to prepare myself for their joke. I decided to act like a normal person at the sound of his name; and I would not react to the joke at all.

Posey: Jean Dancy, you're awfully calm.

Me: (In a monotone, unexcited voice) Yes, I know. Muhammad Ali is going to be on The Tonight Show tonight, right?

Posey: Yes, he is. Somehow I thought you'd be more excited.

Me: How long do you expect me to fall for that joke? Exactly how l-o-n-g?

Posey: Jean Dancy, have I ever played that joke on you? I've actually felt sorry for you sometimes when they played that joke on you. No, he REALLY IS going to be here today, Jean.

Me: Oh, I'm so sure that Muhammad Ali will be here today.

As I walked out of the door, she followed me. They knew that I didn't believe them so they followed me out of the lounge trying to convince me. Posey even ran behind me trying desperately to convince me it was true.

Although I walked out of the lounge calmly…somewhere inside of me, I had to *at least* check it out. I didn't want to call anyone who could possibly be in on the joke. So I went up to the sixth floor (where the show was taped) to see if his name appeared on the dressing room door.

I turned the corner and…THERE IT WAS! His name… MUHAMMAD ALI, big as daaay—on the door!!! People who worked with me understood what I was going through. I fell against the wall. My legs turned to spaghetti and I started crying. I was breathing so rapidly that I didn't know what to do with myself. I had never felt that way before. The day I had really really wanted since I was a child had finally come!!! I remember thinking: I don't think Ali and I should shake hands or touch at all. No hug…nothing. I don't think I could handle that.

I was told by someone from the studio what time he was expected to arrive. I had about four hours to wait, which was good. I needed time to try and get myself together. I don't know why but I started blowing air out of my mouth. I started pacing the floor.

I went downstairs almost an hour early because I wanted to be there—in place—when he entered. I stood against the Information booth like an oak tree. I didn't want company or anyone to talk with me. I just wanted to focus—with no distractions—on Muhammad Ali.

A dream is born—long before it comes alive.

— Jean Dancy

SIX

Dancing on a Cloud

I STOOD THERE…almost floating. Posey was right, it was no joke this time. I had now entered the reality of my biggest dream. The biggest moment of my life had finally come!!!

It was as if the earth stood still and the planets stood in line like elementary school children going to recess. The birds stopped in mid air and there was silence everywhere.

The biggest moment of my life had finally come. Muhammad Ali was actually entering the building!!!

As he walked through the door, he seemed *at least* 10 feet tall!!! And he seemed to have famous spray all over him. Clearly, he was larger than life to me. Seeing him was too much to take in and process at one time. I felt like there was some kind of short circuit going on inside of me. I was breathing more rapidly than ever before, crying and trying to stand up. I didn't know how much longer I could stand. For a moment I felt like a balloon and the helium was about to take me up...up...and awaaay!

I was holding on to the Information booth for dear life! The closer he came to me, the weaker I became. And although my heart was saying, "YES, yes, my dream has finally come true;" I heard my mouth saying, "No...no," as he reached me...and extended his hand toward my left shoulder. It felt like slow motion and I finally said very quickly, "NO, no, Ali, I'm not ready for you to touch me. I don't think I can handle it."

Ali: (Wide-eyed and smiling) Are you going through all of this for me?

I could no longer speak. I just shook my head, yes. He asked my name. I knew I had a name...but gosh, what was it?! After a moment, I managed to remember it. And I told him that I had wanted to meet him all of my life. And that I prayed for him daily.

Ali: (Talking more slowly) Calm down. You can calm down now, Jean. You've met me. And I'm going to take you to dinner with me after I tape the show.

Me: (Weakly) You Aaare?!!

Ali: Yes, I'm taking you to dinner with me. You've wanted to meet me your whole life. You've prayed for me...every day. Don't you think I should do something nice for you too? You can bring one of your friends with you.

I was ecstatic! But having Ali say, "Calm down," actually calmed me down. Reality set in. I had met Muhammad Ali. He had touched my left shoulder. He had given me a big hug! When we reached the sixth floor of the NBC building, people parted like the Red Sea. I worked there. I had seen the biggest names on the planet but I had never seen people react the way they reacted to Ali.

Ali: (Looking around with a raised voice) This young lady is supposed to work in The Tonight Show this evening. Where's her boss? She won't be there. She is going to dinner with me after I tape the show.

Everybody laughed and said it was okay. All of the big executives were out of their offices gazing at Ali. They were in awe of him just like the rest of us. They would have done anything he said.

It was nice that it was okay for me to go to dinner with Muhammad— but I was going anyway. I was working there primarily to meet Ali. I was also prepared to lose a job because of him.

I waited outside of The Tonight Show studio for Ali. He was the first guest and he was leaving immediately after the interview. Because I worked that show, I knew what was going on and how long it should take. I refused to budge. I wouldn't even go down to the mezzanine to get my things from my locker. I sent someone. No matter what, I was going to be in place.

Ali came out after he finished his interview. There were three men with him. A female co-worker who was lucky enough to have been standing close to me—where I was planted like a tree, accompanied us to dinner.

Immediately after we arrived at the restaurant, I told Muhammad that more than anything, I wanted to share that moment with my mother. Momma and I were so close. She was my sweetest, dearest friend. And I adored her. A phone was brought to the table and I called my mother. He and my mother talked for awhile. He told her that she had done a good job with me, that I was a very nice young lady.

Ali: (To my mother) Your daughter is the first woman who ever met me…and also wanted to meet my wife. Your daughter is a very special young lady. She will do great things in life one day.

After my mother and Muhammad finished talking, I asked if he would introduce me to his wife, Kalilah, on the phone. He called home. They lived in Cherry Hill, New Jersey at the time. I spoke with his wife. She was very nice and also very surprised that I wanted to meet her.

Me: Ali, I love you so much that I dislike all of the people that you dislike. I had a chance to meet Joe Frazier when he was a guest on the show, but I refused to meet him.

Ali: I don't dislike Joe Frazier at all. I said all of that stuff to sell the fight. Joe is one of the nicest people you will ever meet. If I could have him for my best friend, I would. If you ever get a chance to meet Joe Frazier again, take it.

It was amazingly comfortable sitting next to Ali talking with him. All of the butterflies in my stomach were asleep. He felt like family to me…like the big brother that I had always imagined he would be. I felt totally connected to him. He and I laughed and talked so freely about boxing and he seemed so interested in *my* life. He wasn't self centered at all; and the dinner wasn't rushed. He allowed me to fully enjoy being in his presence.

Ali: Your mother taught you well…because you're not out here with your body all uncovered. Keep yourself covered up…just like you are today.

Me: Okay, I will.

Ali: Stay in school. Get yourself a good education. And remember that men don't want to see half-naked women out here. They can't respect them. A man wants to use his imagination. Women today don't let men use their imaginations. Stay the way you are…and one day, you'll be a good wife for someone.

It was as if he wanted to send me on my way with words of wisdom from him. He was far more beautiful than I could have ever imagined. Ali walked over to meee, just as I had seen him doing since I was a child. And I loved him sooooo much more than before!

My friends were so happy for me the next day. They kept saying that my biggest dream had come true.

Me: I am so grateful that half of my biggest dream has come true. I still have to have dinner at Ali's house.

They thought I should be satisfied and forget the rest of my dream. Faith had caused him to walk straight over to me…and I knew that the same faith would cause me to have dinner at his house.

A dream will become its own compass.

— Ava Monroe

SEVEN

Moving to L.A.

AS I SAT high in the sky overlooking Los Angeles, looking at the glistening lights below the plane, I knew that destiny would take my hand...and make all of my dreams come true. I heard that Muhammad moved from Cherry Hill, New Jersey to Chicago. I no longer had that desperate, frantic need to meet Ali again. I knew that just as I had actually met him at NBC and just as he had actually taken me to dinner at a restaurant, I would actually have dinner with him at his house.

It was all on God's books. I just had to calmly wait for the manifestation of it. I had a mature, confident knowing deep down inside of me. That feeling was as real to me as the breath that I was breathing. I looked out of the window and said, "Jean Dancy, so-o-o many wonderful things are about to happen to you here." Although I had been guaranteed a job with The Tonight Show in California, I decided not to take it. The show had recently moved from New York to California. I decided to pursue my acting career instead.

I had always spoken things and they came true. That was one of the reasons that I wanted to meet Muhammad Ali. However, I had begun to feel even more like him. He would speak things and they would come true so quickly.

Two very powerful things had happened to me since I met Ali. One happened in New York and the other one happened shortly after I moved to California. I had spoken each one of them into existence. The most pressing one had to do with my personal life. I prayed and told God that I wanted to move away from New York to California.

NBC was sending people from New York to California to work for an extended period of time during a strike. I heard that news a day after I decided I wanted to move from New York to California. I jumped for joy because I felt that was God's way of answering my prayer. I could see the plane ticket in my hand.

NBC (New York) had already sent 10 men to California. I didn't like the fact that women weren't included so I called a meeting with the women to air my feelings. All of them were in agreement with me but they felt powerless to do anything about it. I said, "Let's meet with the administrator who's handling it and let him know that women should also be sent." Nobody wanted to be the spokesperson. I volunteered to speak for us.

Over twenty women gathered in his office when it was time to speak. I spoke to the administrator about how unfair it was for women to be left out. He apologized and said he needed two more people and he would gladly send women.

As they were trying to decide which two women would be sent, I offered my opinion. All of the women wanted to go but there were only two more tickets left.

Me: The only fair thing to do is to go by seniority.

Jennifer: Jean Dancy, we all know that you've been here the longest. No. I think we should put all of the names in a hat and pull the two names from there.

All of the women voted against my idea and the name pulling was scheduled for the following day at noon.

Me: I'm *still* going. This doesn't change anything. I will be on the plane to California at midnight tomorrow night.

I called my best friend, Sandra, and asked if she would check on my apartment for me while I was away. I gave all of my work days away.

Jennifer: Jean, are you saying that your name will come out of the hat tomorrow? There will be at least twenty-two names in the hat.

Me: I'm not saying that my name will come out of the hat. I am only saying that I am going to California tomorrow night. NBC is sending me. They will not leave without me.

A crowd gathered the next day. People from other departments came to see if my name would be pulled. They laughed and said, "Keep Jean Dancy FAR AWAY from the hat and those names!"

Posey held the hat. She took a deep breath, slowly pulled a rolled up name out of the hat, opened it...and shook her head in disbelief.

Posey: People, I'm not lying. It's Jean Dancy's name!

Then she passed the paper around for everyone to see. It didn't surprise me at all. I had not helped fate's hand at all. I had been nowhere near the hat or the names. That was allll God!

Everyone knew that I also wanted Karen Brennan to go with me. The crowd stared at me as if I were Houdini. People started asking, "Is Karen's name coming out of the hat too?" I told them I didn't know.

Posey pulled the final name out of the hat and in an attempt seemingly not to faint, she said, "People...IT'S KAREN! They began to yell in excitement and utter amazement. Posey yelled over them to get their attention.

Posey: Waiiit! It's Karen...but not Karen Brennan! It's Karen Steinberg.

Karen Steinberg called home to ask her mom if she could go. Her mother said that she could not go without supervision. Karen came back and said, "I can't go. I may as well continue in the magic and give my ticket to the one who Jean Dancy wants to go."

So she gave her ticket to my friend, Karen Brennan; and just like that my hopes came true and we were on our way to California!

The second thing I had spoken into existence happened less than a month after I moved to California. My walking on air and positive attitude didn't sit well with everyone in my acting class at Theatrecraft Playhouse on Sunset Blvd. A group of actors were talking about how hard it was to get into the union (The Screen Actors Guild).

Lori: Jean, it could take y-e-a-r-s for you to get into the union. You don't know. You just got here. So stop saying it won't take you that long because you don't know.

Me: There is NO way it will take me y-e-a-r-s to get into the union. It won't even take me a year. In fact, I'll be in the union in less than six months!

They laughed just as they laughed when I told them that one day I would be invited to dinner at Muhammad Ali's house.

Their comments didn't bother me at all. I laughed too. However, in less than 30 days, Fred Williamson had given me a part in a movie; and I was in the union.

Real friendship will outlast time and circumstances.
— Jean Dancy

EIGHT

But Where is Muhammad Ali?

⁓⁓

MY "ON AGAIN—off again" romance with Dennis Edwards was yet again adding sparkles to my life. He had recently moved from Detroit to California and I was so glad. Dennis Edwards was lead singer of the legendary group—The Temptations. That Motown group was one of the most successful and most famous groups in music history.

Though it was shortly after my nineteenth birthday when Dennis and I met, he assumed I was much older. The years between us became apparent when I told him that he had to ask my mother if I could accept his invitation to Detroit. I was in college, still living at home with my mother in Alabama; and I wouldn't have flown to Detroit without her permission. Thank God she gave her permission!

Dennis and I had done our romantic dance for a few years. He was easily the most romantic man I had ever met. He would call and wake me with, "Hello Daar-ling, did you rest well? I'm on my way to hold you in my arms." He would walk through my door, hug and kiss me; and go straight to my piano where he would sing and play love songs to me. I was on *Cloud Nine!*

We would spend the day together and end up at his house; where he would sit at his piano and continue serenading me. Those were some of the best times of my entire life. One time, in particular, stands out to me. Dennis and I were in Detroit at 1300 Lafayette, his residence downtown. It was a lovely high-rise building. And we were high atop the city. It was Christmastime and the city looked like it was covered in a big white blanket as it continued to snow…and snow.

The Temptations had recorded a Christmas album with the song, "Let it Snow" on it. Dennis sang it better than anyone on earth has ever sung it—or ever will sing it—for me.

He scooped me up in his arms as the song started to play and he sang it to me so sweetly and so tenderly. Snowflakes waltzed softly on the outside of his huge windows making their way to the boats and water below on the Detroit river. I can say that I nearly turned into butter! Right there. In his arms. Butter people…butter!!!

Many years later, my daughter---singer, Ava Monroe---sang and toured with Dennis Edwards. He had no idea that she was my daughter when she was hired. How amazing is that?! He was ecstatic to discover that Ava was my daughter and she couldn't wait to reconnect us over the phone. They developed a beautiful bond on tour and the wonderful harmony between Dennis and me was still aparent in our friendship. All of the years bewteen us hadn't distanced us at all.

Life was wonderful for me in every way. I was modeling and acting. My two closest male friends (purely platonic) were movie stars. Women would have paid, at that time, just to *meet* them. By all accounts they were also super good-looking.

I met Philip first. Philip Michael Thomas is best known for his role as detective Ricardo Tubbs on the hit TV series, "Miami Vice." Philip took the first professional pictures of me when I was looking for an agent. He was with me when I sang jazz in public for the first time; and he took me to various events with him.

My other dear friend, Max Julian, is known for starring in the movie, "The Mack." He is also a writer and producer. Max and I would sit and talk for hours…and hours about love, about life, about philosophy and so many things. Although Max and I found each other very attractive, we never dated. Instead, we enjoyed our perfect friendship chemistry.

All of this…But where is Muhammad Ali?

Muhammad Ali is alive and well and living less than 10 minutes from me.

Love is instant. It never has to be brewed.

— Jean Dancy

NINE

Meeting Marty Monroe

THOUGH I DIDN'T know it, my life was about to change more quickly than the sand in an hourglass. Things had begun to come to me so easily in terms of my career. I was grateful to be a member of the Screen Actors Guild (SAG), to have been in a movie, and I had begun to be quite busy modeling.

Someone from the Cunningham Agency (William D. Cunningham and Associates) in Beverly Hills had seen my picture. The agency called me in and asked if I would allow them to represent me as a model. I hadn't even thought about modeling. Though about 5'8, I wasn't considered short, I thought I needed to be taller to become a model.

After I signed with Cunningham, I started to do Print work immediately. I did ads for milk, beer, More Cigarettes, the Marriott

Hotel, and the list went on. I did a big ad for Smirnoff's Vodka and posters with my picture on them were hanging from the ceilings in liquor stores.

I had begun to travel. And although Dennis and I lived in the same city, with his career and mine, his traveling and mine, we rarely saw each other. Even when I was home and he wanted to send for me, most of the time I was no longer available to go.

Keeping each other as close friends became our new goal. And we achieved it. We were actually able to laugh and talk about the people that we were dating! Crazy, though it may seem (at least on my part!), Dennis and I were both very excited about his dates with Aretha Franklin. I love her voice sooo much! She is my favorite singer and I loved hearing about how she was as a person. I was actually cheering for her! According to Aretha, Dennis was the reason that she wrote the song, *"Day Dreaming."* As for Dennis Edwards, our special bond and golden friendship never tarnished with time.

It's amazing how one moment in time—just *one*—can change who you are—and who you will forever be. It's a defining moment that puts a wonderful stamp on your life…for the rest of your life.

Such a moment was waiting for me…and whispering to me but I couldn't hear it. I could almost feel it though…like a magical magnet pulling…trying to take me to the top of a mountain that I had never seen. A place where the air is rare. And most people *never* get there.

I was just minutes away from entering into a realm of life located on the outskirts of heaven. I was already happy, very happy, and extremely grateful. But I was about to go even higher. Much higher! I was about to enter an existence where angels put things together and where God's Fingerprints could be seen and felt on everything happening. I didn't know to fasten my seat belt because I had no idea that I would get there so quickly!

I went to party given by a songwriter for Diana Ross; and my life was forever changed…in one night…in one magic moment. Destiny swooped in like a lovely dove from heaven…and took my hand… and my entire life in a different direction.

Undefeated Heavyweight boxer, Marty Monroe, was there. A boxer at the party (who was trying to get rid of me so that he could talk to my friend) actually took Marty Monroe by the hand, pulled him in front of me, left and chased my friend. Marty just stood there. After a few moments of awkward silence, I spoke.

Me: So, you must be the boxer, Marty Monroe?

Marty: (So politely) Yes, I am.

(More moments of silence)

Me: So, how long have you been boxing?

Marty: Well, I actually started boxing when I was only 5 years old.

Me: (Really interested) So, why did you start boxing at such an early age? Other little boys were playing cowboys or marbles at that age.

He shared so much with me; including the fact that he was about to sign a management contract with Joe Frazier. After I had asked him at least 102 questions, he asked me a few questions.

Marty: Was NBC upset with you when you refused to talk to Joe Frazier?

Me: (Wondering why he asked that question) No. NBC didn't mind. But Muhammad Ali told me that Joe Frazier was the most wonderful person, a great man, and that I should talk with him if I ever get the chance again.

Marty: Ali is right about Joe Frazier. Joe is one of the best people you could ever meet. Wow! You started at the top...talking with Muhammad Ali.

Me: I'll never forget the day I got a chance to ask Ali some of my boxing questions.

Marty: You're not taping this or taking notes. Are you going to remember everything that I've said?

Me: Yes, I have a great memory. An incredible memory. But why would I tape this or take notes?

Marty: You...being a reporter and all...

Me: A REPORTER? I'm not a reporter!

Marty: (Looking so puzzled) You're not? You're not the reporter scheduled to interview me at this party?

Me: (Laughing) Nooo, I'm not!

Marty: (Nicely…but a little embarrassed) Then why did you ask me so many questions?

Me: Because it was so interesting!

A journalist at the party was scheduled to interview him. By a "divine" mix-up, he thought I was the woman waiting to interview him.

We talked over 30 minutes before he discovered that I was not the woman interviewing him. I can understand his confusion though; because I asked so many questions about his boxing career and about his life.

He politely apologized to me and gently walked away. His smooth personality left a wonderful fragrance with me.

The party was so "Hollywood." I heard every conceivable "line" from men who were trying to get my phone number. I just wanted to be left alone. So I eased into a room near the entrance of the lovely home. About 10 minutes later Marty came to the door and asked if he could share something with me.

Marty: There's something I *need* to tell you.

Me: (Jokingly) I don't think you've known me long enough to *need* to tell me anything. You mean there's something that you *want* to tell me?

Marty: No, I actually *need* to tell you something. I don't know any other way to say it…but to just say it.

Me: Say what?

Marty: Okay, you're my wife!

Me: Your WIFE?!!!

Marty: My search is over. I always said, "I will know her when I see her," and you're it. You're my wife. (Pointing to my fingers) Those are my wife's fingers. Your voice is my wife's voice. You are my wife.

His words were shocking to say the least. However, I felt like I had known him for at least 100 years and I was more comfortable with him than anyone I had ever known. Something inside of me knew instinctively that he was speaking from his heart. His words flowed with total sincerity.

After we talked for about 20 minutes, he leaned over to kiss me. I turned my head and he kissed the side of my face so sweetly and so tenderly. About 10 minutes later, he asked if he could hug me.

Marty: May I hug you…please? I just need to know how it feels to hug my wife.

He stood up in front of me. I stood up. We hugged. In that hug…in that moment, I knew that I would *never* leave him. I knew *then* that only death could separate us. I felt that his body was poured into mine. We were one. Instantly. That quickly!

Me: This is the hug that I have wanted all of my life. I could never leave this hug.

Marty: You just hugged your husband, baby.

I didn't need time to get to know him. I knew him instantly and intimately—without any sex. I felt that our hearts had been woven together by God. Marty's hug felt permanent, like it was the hug that would never leave me.

I felt that we existed in God's Mind before the foundation of the world was formed, before Adam and Eve. I felt that we always had been…and that we always would be. With tears in his eyes, he asked me to marry him—*that* night. And with tears in my eyes, I knew I would.

Love doesn't need a key.

— Jean Dancy

TEN

Life with Marty

THE NEXT DAY he took me to the boxing gym with him. I felt so at home there. It was as if a part of me lived there and it was just waiting for me to return. That must have been how Betty Crocker felt when she discovered baking. I was home.

After about three months, a veteran in the boxing business, Cannon Ball, said, "You talk boxing as well as any of the men in here. Where did you come from?"

The energy in the Hoover Street Gym was electric and so exciting. I didn't ever want to leave.

Marty and I were together every day. Being in the boxing gym with him was the highlight of my day. When he finished training he taught me about the sport of boxing and all of the terminology used. Although teaching me really fed his ego, I was thirsty to know everything. Our lives were totally interwoven. He went with me on modeling assignments. And I went to business meetings with him. I would recap all that had been said in the meetings for him. I took care of all of his business.

At one shinning moment in time, Marty Monroe was an undefeated Heavyweight boxer…a prized commodity at the time. Marty had one of the best teams in boxing history: The legendary, Eddie Futch, said to be the best trainer in the world; gifted trainer, Thell Torrance; and the legendary, Joe Frazier, as his manager.

Because of Muhammad Ali, my heart was open to Joe Frazier's friendship. And Ali was right, Joe was an absolutely beautiful person. Marty and I went to big parties with Joe and legendary boxer, Ken Norton. Joe Frazier used to take Marty and me to hang out with him in Vegas, where he showered us with kindness and generosity.

With Joe as Marty's manager and promises of consistent fights, Marty was on a cloud! However, almost two years later, Marty was miserable. The main source of his misery was inactivity.

I had read the contract that would make Joe Frazier Marty's manager and I begged Marty not to sign it. Joe was a beautiful man who was not handling the "day-to-day" business. We loved Joe but the contract wasn't working for Marty. Only one fight in almost two years was depressing.

Marty: (Concerning the contract with Joe Frazier) Baby, I guess you wanna say, "I told you so." But I wouldn't listen. I had just met you and Thell is like a father to me. I have known him since I was a little boy. I just couldn't go against him. I hadn't known you long enough to know how smart you are. Say it. Say, "I told you so."

Me: Darling, I have no desire to say that to you. I have just one question. Would you like for me to get you out of the contract this week?

Marty: GET ME OUT OF IT?!!! THIS WEEK? HOW?! But I thought I had to be in that contract for years.

Me: They've already breached the contract. I can get you out of it.

We met with a very high-powered sports attorney who was working with some of the Lakers. We gave him my copy of Marty's contract where I had made notes on the side. There were 11 things that I wanted changed on the contract.

Attorney: Marty, if you had made the changes that your other attorney wrote on here, you would have a perfect contract.

Marty: (Totally shocked!) But Jean wrote those things!

Attorney: Lady, you missed your calling. You would have been a great attorney. How did you understand the contract so well?

Me: I was an English teacher. I read and comprehend words very well. That's all.

After I got Marty out of that contract, I could do no wrong in his eyes. He listened to *everything* I said about business, from then on.

After making a clean break from his renowned team, Marty and I had no idea what we would do next. Marty had wanted so badly to keep Thell Torrance and Eddie Futch as his trainers; but things just didn't work out that way.

After Marty and I were newly married, we were riding down Wilshire Blvd. singing love songs to each other. And someone followed us honking frantically on the horn until we pulled over. The man yelled, "Marty Monroe, Muhammad Ali is looking for you! Man, take this number and call him. They don't have your number."

Marty was in such transition where his career was concerned. So we were ecstatic and eager to find out what Ali wanted. By that time, I had negotiated a car accident on Marty's behalf. I had gotten him money that his attorney couldn't even get him; And I had also gotten him out of two seemingly ironclad boxing contracts. However, Marty still needed a trainer, a manager, and a promoter.

Our lives may have been in mid-air where my husband's career was concerned; however, our personal lives couldn't have been on more solid ground. Life with Marty was better than anything I had ever heard about or read about. We lived on the outskirts of heaven. I felt bathed in warm honey and our days were filled with lots of hugs and kisses and laughter.

I remember making a list about the kind of husband I wanted. But God gave me three times more than my heart's desire. We were like magnets. Always touching each other. Always holding hands. It's as if we were in a contest with each other—to see who could treat the other one better.

Marty would leave home and call me back from his car phone, "Baby, do you have any idea how fiiine you are? You're what's called qualified. You're smart…and pretty…and sexy. And you love God! People wonder how I pulled this off. They wonder how I got you, baby."

He was sooo romantic. He sang love songs to me everyday. (By the way, he was from a musical family and he could actually sing!) We danced together, sang together, prayed together, and our home life was so exciting.

He showered me with love and attention from the time I woke up until I fell asleep in his arms.

We'd ride down the street, he would see a man selling roses on the corner, buy them and pull one rose out for me. Then he'd pull over and give the rest of them to a lady on the bus stop. Sometimes the women would cry in appreciation to him.

He complimented me all the time, about the way I looked to him and for the least little thing I did for him. I felt so appreciated; and it made me want to show him how I felt—about how he made *me* feel! When he walked through the door at home I took his shoes off and I served him royally for the rest of the evening. He was my king, my everything. I lived to serve God and then to serve my husband.

He never saw me push a vacuum, clean or do anything like that. I gave him my undivided attention in our marriage, as I did when we were dating. I did all cleaning and cooking (except breakfast) when he was away from home or asleep. Never when he was awake and at home.

He always acted as if he had stolen the queen and he wanted to enjoy me before they caught him—and took me back to the palace.

I felt loved, and honored, and adored, and appreciated—daily! That was the fuel that made me want to do everything that I could do for Marty. Therefore, when we heard that Muhammad Ali was looking for Marty—I was even happier for my husband than I was for myself. Imagine that! I knew it had to be something good for Marty.

The steps of a good man are ordered
by The Lord.
— Psalm 37:23 (KJV)

ELEVEN

Destiny is Calling

SANTA MONICA, CALIFORNIA. We found out that Muhammad Ali had started promoting boxers. His company was scooping up all of the most elite boxers and signing them to his company, MAPS: Muhammad Ali Professional Sports. His roster already included Tommy "Hit Man" Hearns, Tony Tubbs, and Eddie Mustafa Muhammad, just to name a few.

I tried to imagine what it would be like seeing Ali's face again but nothing came up on the screen in my mind. It had been a few years since I met Muhammad Ali at NBC. I had an entirely new look and I was different in every way. I was no longer that teenage young lady filled with helium. I was a woman now but I loved Ali as much as I ever had.

Since I met Ali, I had gotten a B.S. degree in English and Psychology. I had gotten married to the man of my dreams. And I was a newlywed!

When Harold Smith stopped Marty in traffic that day, I was actually even more excited for my husband to meet with Ali than I was for myself. Marty really needed a new team. I was working daily reading contracts, trying to find the best managerial contract for my husband.

I knew there would be a rush seeing Ali's face again. There would *have* to be! But I would not attempt to take a bite out of his arm or grab his ankles. I was a businesswoman now and I had to conduct myself accordingly.

When we entered the office building, Marty wanted to say, "Hello," to Ali before we picked up the contract. Within seconds Muhammad Ali was before my eyes again! It was as if someone had captured the sun and put it in a room. It was high, high voltage. He was still larger than life to me, bigger than people, and things and…WOW! I wanted to tap dance, beat the drums, and blow a trumpet. But I knew that was not the time nor the place for what I felt going on inside of me. I appeared calm and collected. There was a smile frozen on my face because I loved Ali so much. I still prayed for him daily and I still felt like he was family to me.

After Marty introduced me and told him that we were newlyweds, Ali looked at me all wide-eyed.

Ali: Every boxer ought to have a pretty wife. Man, she is gor-ge-ous!

Marty: This woman is pretty AND smart. She is *real* smart.

Ali joked about boxers being smart enough to get pretty women. Then he invited Marty to train with him in his Santa Monica gym.

Ali: Marty you should train in my gym all the time. It's clean *and* we feed you. There's a cook there right now.

Then we picked up the contract from Lee (Harold Smith's wife).

Marty: (To Lee) My wife will look over the contract and she'll make an appointment for us to come back.

I had been amazingly quiet. I felt that if I talked, all of the excitement inside of me would cause me to fly around the office like a bird!

God has a way of bringing your gifts out—long before Christmas.
— Jean Dancy

TWELVE

Sign on the Dotted Line

I DIDN'T WANT to eat or sleep. All I wanted to do was taste that contract from Ali's office and hope it was delicious. It was not. But it could be fixed with some good seasonings and a cup of sugar. The contract from his office was better than any of the others that I had seen.

The most recent contract that I had gotten Marty out of had prepared me for all contracts to come. I would not allow Marty to make ANY of the same mistakes twice. There was only one clause that could break the whole deal for me and I would not budge on it. That clause was one of the most major reasons why Marty was inactive with the Joe Frazier contract.

I went over the contract with our attorney. Told him exactly how I wanted him to handle each part. I felt totally confident that things would go very smoothly. Armed with what I told him about boxing, along with his own expertise as a lawyer, I saw a home-run.

It doesn't matter how great an attorney is, if he doesn't understand how the boxing business works—he's at a disadvantage.

When we arrived, Ali wasn't in his office but later, I heard people whispering, "Ali is here. Ali is here." No matter how often they saw him, he was *still* Muhammad Ali.

Having a degree in English gave me confidence when it came to reading and comprehending contracts. However, I knew it would be good business to take a very high-powered sports attorney with us to the meeting. Marty, our attorney, and I were seated in an office waiting for Harold Smith (the promoter in charge of the boxers) and for the attorney representing Ali's company.

The meeting started out pleasantly enough. However, I didn't know there would be such tooth pulling. An hour or so later, voices were raised and I could feel the tension in the room. There was no anesthesia and I had begun to hurt. Really hurt. The two attorneys were boxing each other verbally in loud tones. Harold stood up to try to get things back in order.

Maybe I was in La-La land. I actually thought we would go through things quietly and in a civil manner. The contract would be signed. Marty and I would pick up his big signing bonus check and we would go out to dinner and celebrate. Not so. The train was running wildly off the track and nobody could find the conductor! Marty and I sat there holding hands on "mute." Our attorney stood up and shouted, "WELL WE DON'T HAVE A DEAL THEN. WE CAN JUST WALK!"

My thoughts: *Whaaat?!!! We can just walk! Oh nooo we can't. And leave Marty without a promoter. And leave that signing bonus check on the table. Oh n-o-o-o-o! There will be no walking. Not on my watch.*

There was only ONE thing left to negotiate—ONE THING—and we could just walk?!!

That one thing though—was the one thing in cement. I told our attorney that I would not compromise on that one clause. However, I expected our attorney to FIND a way to make it happen for us. I wanted to see our very expensive attorney do some very expensive negotiating. Not just give up!

I felt like toothpaste as I watched them squeeze…and squeeze… and squeeze! Until I just couldn't take much more. This was my husband's life—and my life—that they were kicking around like a football. Then I felt like a volcano. I couldn't take one more second of it. I whispered to Marty:

Me: Darling, would you please ask them to stop the meeting for a minute? I need to speak with you outside.

Once we were beyond their hearing I told him how I felt.

Me: I don't like the way this meeting is going. I know I can make this deal. I've wanted to say something from the beginning but I didn't want to do it without your permission.

Marty: Say whatever you want to say. You know I don't have a problem with that.

Back inside the meeting I told our attorney I would take it from there. You could tell by the look on our attorney's face that he thought I had lost my mind. He was incredulous! As I began to speak, he interrupted me, "Whose side are you on? You sound like you're on their side."

I spoke calmly and politely...though authoritatively. I started out praising them for all of the things that they were willing to give Marty. I was not combative at all, in fact, I was nice. In less than 20 minutes Marty signed the contract. He picked up his signing bonus check and we left. Our attorney was disgusted! His hopes of later becoming Marty's manager were dashed completely. His running out of creative and logical gas in the meeting had left that dream stranded.

Once we left the office, beyond their sight or hearing, Marty lifted me above his head and exploded with joy!

Marty: Baby, you're cold blooded! You. Are. COLD blooded. And so sweet with it. I love it. Don't look at another contract because YOU ARE MY MANAGER!!!

Me: Darling, I'm your wife. I will be by your side—no matter what. I don't have to be your manager. I will see to it that things are handled properly anyway.

Marty: No-o-o-o-o, look what you just did! YOU made that deal happen. You're my manager. I feel better with you handling all of it. Everything. Nobody out there can outtalk you. That's for sure. I know that. Find out what you need to do to become my manager.

I couldn't wait to call my mother and see what she would say about Marty wanting me to be his manager. She was famous for saying, "If you know of anybody else who has ever done it—that's proof that it can be done. You can do it too." My sister, Bonnie, and I had heard that all of our lives.

I was a little nervous when I called her because I didn't know of any other woman who had done what I was about to do. I seriously wondered what she would say.

Me: Momma, Marty wants me to become his manager…and before you say it—I don't know of any other woman who has ever done this.

Momma: Oh darling, that's simple. You will show them how it's done. You will do it with excellence and class. I know you, you will do your homework. You will know much more than you need to know. I'm excited for you…I know you can do it!

Tears eased down my face as she talked…and it felt like she was putting even more confidence into my veins. My mother always rose to the occasion. She was so positive and so beautiful in every way. I simply adored her.

The conversation with my mother that day was a very pivotal one. My life was about to go in either one direction or the other.

My mother believed that Jesus would be a flashlight in any dark situation; and if I ran into questions that I could not answer—all I had to do was pray and get guidance.

Armed with my mother's advice, I was ready to march forth and help Marty.

I took a test at the California State Athletic Commission. Passed the test and got my license to manage boxers. Marty and I signed contracts like we were strangers. He and I both wanted it that way.

Me: Marty, I need only ONE promise from you.

Marty: You got it baby, whatever it is.

Me: Darling, in our marriage, your word is the final word. And I have no problem with that. I wouldn't have married you if I could not respect your decisions. But as your manager, I need to know that MY word is the final word—on everything. No matter what anyone else has to say.

Marty: Is that all you want? You got that, baby. You had that anyway.

"Float like a butterfly, sting like a bee."
— Bundini Brown

THIRTEEN

Bundini

"FLOAT LIKE A butterfly, sting like a bee." Those words have been heard all over the world and I wanted to meet the man who created them—Bundini Brown. Like Ali, he was a poet. Always creating interesting things with words. Jamie Foxx played him in the movie, "Ali" starring Will Smith.

He's known affectionately as the "loud mouth" in Ali's corner. He was there in the office building when we were negotiating Marty's contract but we didn't get a chance to see him. I knew that being around Ali, also meant that I would be around Bundini as well. However, I had no preparation…none…for how he actually was.

Immediately after the contract was signed Marty and I left the office and went to a fight at the Forum. Our dear friend, Tony Curtis, put on exciting boxing events for the Forum. I loved boxing and watching it with Marty made it three times more exciting. As we were leaving the Forum, I saw Bundini Brown. He was walking very swiftly ahead of the crowd. I didn't realize he was so tall. Marty was about 6'4 and Bundini seemed almost that tall as well. I really wanted to meet him.

Me: Marty…Marty…there's Bundini Brown!

At that moment, Bundini turned around and looked at us.

Bundini: Marty Mon-roe! The Philadelphia Spectrum. C.J. Bar Brown. Man, that knockout was sweet…and quick. You got a wicked right hand and so much heart.

Marty: Ah, man…thank you.

Bundini: Marty, who is this pretty woman you got with you? She looks just like one of Ray Robinson's pretty wives.

We shook hands with Bundini and Marty introduced me as his brand new wife.

Bundini: Where y'all headed? You hungry? Let me take you out to eat, Marty. Your pretty wife can choose the restaurant.

By then we were really hungry. I told him that I wanted breakfast food and it didn't matter where we ate. I asked Bundini to pick the place. He took us to a restaurant in Beverly Hills that stayed open late.

I had wanted to meet Bundini for years so I was very excited at the thought of sitting down talking with him. We sat at a plush leather booth. Marty and I sat side-by-side and Bundini sat directly across from us. Before our food arrived, I fixed Marty's coffee—cream, sugar, and a tiny dash of salt. I tasted it and gave it to Marty. Then I fixed mine.

When the waiter brought our food, I buttered Marty's toast and put a thin layer of strawberry preserves on it. I put a tiny bit of salt and pepper on his eggs and his hash brown potatoes. Tasted the food and gave it to Marty.

Bundini: I've never seen anything like this before. (Looking at me like I had just landed from Mars) You gon' eat it for him too? Marty, where did you find *her*? From now on, I'm gonna call you "Lil' Mamma, Lil' Mamma."

We laughed so hard at the table that people kept looking at us...and laughing with us. Bundini was so funny and people seemed happy to see him in person.

After Marty explained his need for a manager and a trainer, Bundini offered his view on how Marty had me choosing those key people for him.

Bundini: Marty, people don't put their wives out there...running everything...like you doing. A lot of men...got a problem with that. I say, let her do whatever she's big enough to do. I can see...just from tonight how smart she is. Lil' Mamma always talk like this? This *proper*? Is she picking everybody you working with?

Marty: My wife is handling everything. And I'm gonna work with whoever she picks and I'm gonna sign wherever she says sign. This woman has done so much for my life. I-love-her-so-much.

Bundini: Without a trainer, you gon' need somebody in your corner. I got boxers pulling at me left and right...but I wanna work with you, Marty. (A long pause...) That is...if it's okay with Lil' Mamma.

After having watched Bundini in Ali's corner since Marty was a little boy, Marty wanted to see what it would be like working with him too. I was in total agreement with Bundini working with Marty. We shook hands on it.

Marty: People can say whatever they wanna say about this woman. But my wife just settled a case for me against an attorney... an ATTORNEY...And she got my money within two days!

Bundini: How'd you do that, Lil' Mamma?

Me: I just spoke his language. That's all. I assured him that the Bar Association would be very interested in his fraudulent activities. I pointed out how many clients he would lose—and how many clients he would never gain if I went public with the information.

As we were leaving the restaurant, Bundini asked the manager if he could see the chef. When the chef came out Bundini put a $100 dollar bill in his hand. He had already tipped the waiter. Bundini explained that the waiter gets all the tips but the chef does all the work. When the food is good, Bundini said he always tips the chef as well.

Marty and I spent the next few days hanging out with Bundini. He and his lady, Easy, invited us over for dinner. Bundini cooked the best roasted duck and wild rice that I have ever tasted in my life! He could have been a top chef anywhere. Easily.

My number one priority was to get Marty's career back on track. I had not turned by back on my career, I had a *new* career! I felt good about having Bundini with us; but I was still looking for a trainer who would be with Marty on a day-to-day basis as well. Later, I hired veteran trainer, Bill Slayton (best known for training Ken Norton) to work with Marty along with Bundini.

Tony Curtis and Bill Slayton could be trusted. When it came to business with them, a handshake was always good enough.

Though I was being called for modeling and acting jobs, I gladly put my career on hold. I gave 100% of my time to getting Marty's boxing career situated---properly. Some people thought I was crazy. But I was doing *exactly* what I wanted to do.

Royalty is appointed by God. It's in your voice, your smile...your fingerprints.

— Jean Dancy

FOURTEEN

Summoned by the King

THE NEXT DAY we got a phone call:

Bundini: Hey, Lil' Mamma. Tell Marty the Champ wants to see y'all at his house this evening. I'll pick y'all up.

A million butterflies flooded my stomach.

Me: Marty, can you believe that?!!! WE have been invited to Muhammad Ali's house! "I" have been invited to *Muhammad Ali's* house.

Marty: (Calmly, with both arms around me) Yes, baby…I can believe that.

Me: Oh my gosh! Aren't you excited? We have been invited to Muhammad Ali's house, Marty. Okay…how many people—on earth—get invited to Muhammad Ali's house? How many, Marty?!!

When we got there Muhammad was sitting at a very regal looking desk. He seemed very happy to see us as he was getting off of the phone. Again, it was like the sun had been captured and put in one room. His face lit up and there was a twinkle in his eyes.

Bundini sat near the massive fireplace and Marty and I sat left of the desk. After greeting each other and settling down a bit, Ali wanted to talk about what happened with the contract.

Ali: Call me back. I've got company.

Bundini: Who was that Champ?

Ali: A king.

Bundini: (Who had not heard him clearly) Don King?

Ali: No. A king.

Me: Are you talking about an *actual* king?

Ali: Yes. Kings call me all the time. He'll call back.

Muhammad told us from what country the king was calling; but I was in such awe of Ali and the whole situation that I was speechless.

Ali was so calm and casual about the king calling. No different than if he had been talking with cousin Bubba from across town. What a way to start our visit!

Ali: I heard what happened with Marty's contract.

Bundini: Champ, I thought your attorney and Marty's attorney were gonna put on gloves and knock each other out. It got loud in there!

Ali: (Wide-eyed) Was it that bad? I had to leave.

Bundini: I was right outside the door. It was that bad. Anybody coulda heard them. Then Lil' Mamma asked Marty if she could take over and handle it. About 15 minutes later…the contract was signed!

Ali: They said she was smooth too. No bad words. No hollering. I like that. I don't like it when women think they have to act like men.

Marty: She blew my mind too! Our attorney said we could just walk…but my wife wasn't having that.

Ali: (To Me) How did you learn to do business like that?

Me: I don't think raising your voice raises your point. I don't use profanity so….

Ali: Marty, Where did you get *her*?

Marty: Man…she's a gift from God. I-love-her-so-much.

Me: And Ali, I wasn't going to leave your office without making that deal for my husband. I just wanted to help Marty.

The evening felt natural, like we had always been friends. I wasn't nervous at all. We talked about poetry. Ali shared a few of his poems with us and I shared a couple of the poems I had written. We talked about boxing and Ali and I went back and forth like a tennis match.

Marty and Bundini chimed in a little bit. I was surprised that Bundini didn't chime in more but he loved seeing my nerve talking to Ali.

Bundini: (Laughing) Champ, Lil' Mamma won't back down will she? Not even for you.

When we got ready to leave Ali wasn't ready for us to go.

Ali: (To Bundini) Bring them back tomorrow. We have to do this again.

Ali gave us his phone number. What a night! That was the beginning of our times at Ali's house. After I had the number for about a week, I called. Ali answered.

Me: Why did you answer the phone?

Ali: (Laughing) Who else is supposed to answer?

Me: (Laughing) I don't know. But I don't expect Muhammad Ali to answer his own phone.

Ali: What's Marty doing? Come over here and talk.

About an hour later Marty and I went over to Ali's house.

Ali's children, Hana and Laila, (both under age 6) would often run in, Ali would hug and kiss them and they would run out. Hana would put her little arm around Ali's neck and just sit there as he talked. She acted like Ali was her favorite teddy bear rather than her dad.

She acted like he belonged to her and she seemed to absolutely adore him.

In the middle of his conversations he'd plant big, big kisses on Hana's face. Laila seemed shy sometimes when he would try to kiss her and she would run away. He would get up and chase her like he was a big child. He clearly adored those little girls. On a scale from 1-10, I would have to give Ali a 10—in terms of being an affectionate, playful, adoring dad.

Hana and Laila's mother, Veronica (One of the most beautiful women I have ever seen), is a poised, gracious, intelligent, articulate woman. I liked her from the moment we met. She seemed to have mastered the art of allowing people to have their time with Ali; or more precisely…for Ali to have his time with people.

Veronica: Jean, Muhammad will not want you and Marty to leave. If you absolutely have to go, you will have to be firm with him.

Firm with him?! He didn't want us to leave; and I didn't want to leave. Marty had to be the referee and stop our wonderful verbal sparring matches.

I was living the life that I always imagined for myself. I was married to the man of my dreams; and I was friends with Muhammad Ali. For me, that was the cake, the icing, and the whipped cream! And I was constantly thanking God.

Faith is the substance of things hoped for,
the evidence of things not seen.
— Hebrews 11:1 (KJV)

FIFTEEN

Guess Who's Coming to Dinner

THE SMELL OF coffee filled the air. I cooked a big breakfast. Turkey ham, turkey bacon, eggs, and I even cooked my sister, Bonnie's, famous home-fried potatoes. I made toast and I browned it in the oven so that it would be married to the butter. As I put the old-fashioned strawberry preserves on Marty's toast he wondered why I wasn't eating.

Marty: You're not eating?

Me: No. I'm saving my appetite for this evening. I want to be really hungry when we eat.

Marty: They want us there at 5 p.m.

Me: What do you think they will have for dinner?

Marty: (Smiling) Probably food.

Me: Darling, I wonder if other people will be there.

Marty: Baby, *you'll* be there.

Me: I know, but I want us to sit close to the man of the house so we can talk over dinner.

Marty Monroe was never…ever…late. So at 5 o'clock we were there. On the way I was almost hungry enough to stop and get a sandwich but I was determined to save my appetite.

We finally arrived. When we walked in, Ali looked so regal and wonderful sitting there smiling radiantly. He was always up to something so in a flash he could be up shadow boxing with Marty, doing magic tricks, reciting poetry, or setting me up for our next verbal sparring match.

The three of us had fun talking. Ali was one of the few people who could really make Marty laugh.

Ali: I sent a car to pick up Veronica.

My thoughts: *Whaat?! You sent a car to pick up Veronica? I hope she's right around the corner because I'm hungry enough to eat a chair!*

Me: Oh...

Ali: She'll be at the airport. This time of day...with traffic and all it'll be pretty late before she gets here. Edith (Ali's cook) says we'll be eating in just a few minutes.

Their dining room table reminded me of the one in the picture of Jesus and the disciples. Ali sat at the head of the table that night and Marty sat at the end of the table closest to Ali's left. I sat beside Marty to my husband's left. When Edith, his cook, started bringing the food out it was apparent that there were no other guests. Yaaaaay!

I will never forget what we had for dinner because it was one of my favorite meals. I'm sure I would have remembered it anyway though. I had wanted this dinner at Ali's house since I was a child. We had a very colorful green salad, all dark green and purple leaves, golden brown baked chicken, macaroni and cheese, fresh string beans, and buttery, buttery home-made monkey bread! Dee-liscious! The bread was so good that I could have just had it—alone—for dinner. It was well worth the wait! Ali told us that his cook was known for that bread. She said we were two of her favorite guests and she even offered to give me the recipe so I could make the bread for Marty. She was as warm as the bread and so nice.

Eating dinner at Muhammad Ali's house was amazingly comfortable. It was a long slow dinner with lots of conversation and we spilled laughter all over the table. Somewhere during dinner, I realized that I didn't have any butterflies in my stomach. It was not apparent that

I was having dinner with the most famous man in the world. It felt familiar and wonderful like I had always imagined.

I felt such love and acceptance at that table. I felt that I belonged there…in Ali's house and at his dinner table. It didn't feel like I had won a lottery to be there or that I was there by chance. It felt the way I said it would feel when I was growing up. I always felt that I would have the kind of sparkling life that would inspire Muhammad Ali to invite me to dinner at his home.

All of the food was delicious; and I ate the way I would have eaten at my grandmother's house. No little pinky finger in the air pretending that I was not hungry. I held that chicken leg the way I held it at home. And I just couldn't get enough of that monkey bread! Ali commented on how *real* Marty and I were. And he was right. I was drawn to Ali when I was a child because he was so real. Ali bathed in being himself and he didn't care who knew it or what they thought about it. As a woman, I was drawn to Marty for the same reason.

After we finished eating and talking for a while, Edith served dessert. By then I was ready to eat it. She had prepared a warm fresh fruit compote. It was nice and light…and perfect.

My dream had come true!!! I had touched it…and hugged it…and it felt like the rest of my life—perfectly wonderful.

I had spent so many hours in my bedroom located on the third floor of our home. I lived a fantasy life in my room with the white French furniture that my mother allowed me to choose. Along with dreams of wanting to get to know Ali, I had dreams about meeting and getting married to a gorgeous hunk of a man, a tall man. A man that I would travel with and do business with. Our marriage would be romantic and perfect for us. We would actually live the marital fairy-tale.

As Marty and I were leaving Ali's house holding hands...we were always holding hands, I realized in that moment that I was Cinderella. However, I didn't have any evil step-sisters and my glass slippers allowed me to walk on air. At midnight my fairy-tale wouldn't end. At midnight, I'd be snuggled up in the arms of...not Prince Charming...but in the arms of my very own king...Marty Monroe. I loved my life!

First time meeting Ali in New York City.

Dennis Edwards and me. (Lead singer of the Temptations)

Heavyweight Boxer, Marty Monroe

Fun in Vegas with my amazing husband, Marty.

Bundini Brown and me (after one of the fights that I promoted).

With Smokin' Joe Frazier in Vegas.

Marty Monroe and Bundini Brown in the ring after a fight.

Ali and me, my first week at Deer Lake Camp.

Fun talking with Ali at Deer Lake Camp.

Sitting on top of the world at Deer Lake Camp with my darling husband, Marty Monroe.

With Marty, petting Hana and Laila Ali's ponies at Deer Lake Camp.

Jean Dancy, Boxing Promoter.

Being interviewed after becoming a Boxing Promoter.

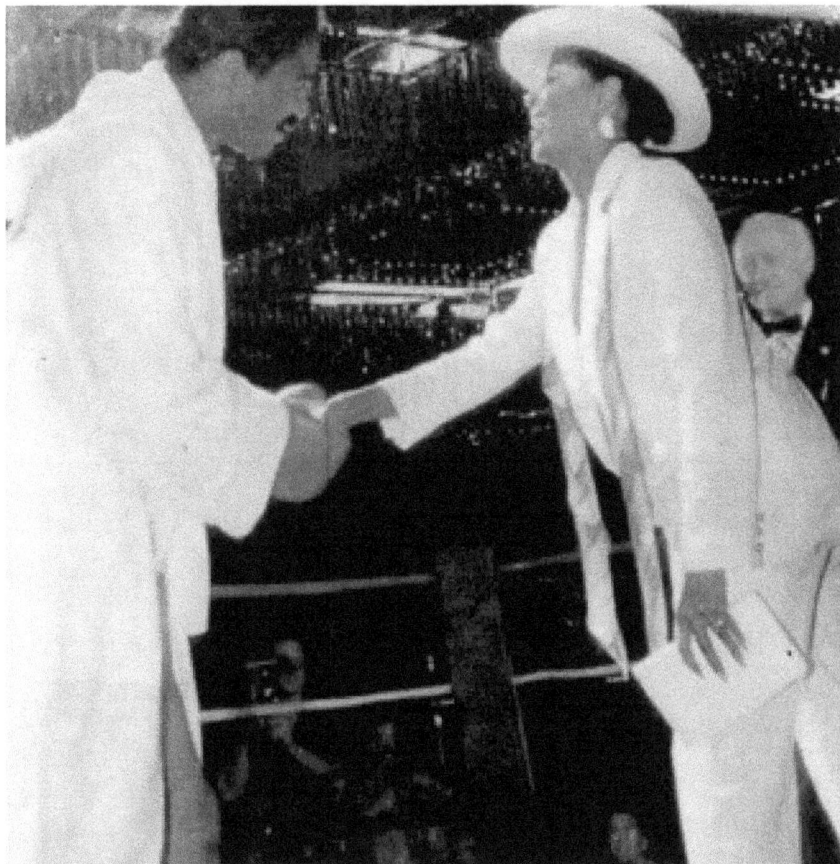

Marty Monroe, Jean Dancy, and Announcer, Jimmy Lennon. The first fight that I promoted for Marty!

Ali and Marty joking around.

My daughter, Ava, and Ali. He said, "You look just like your daddy!"

With Muhammad Ali at his private birthday party; Chasen's restaurant in Beverly Hills, California.

With Tommy "Hitman" Hearns at Ali's private birthday party.

Norton, Ali, and me, having fun at an event for Ali.

With Don King, ringside at a championship fight.

Ringside with President Bob Lee of the IBF (International Boxing Federation), and

President Jose Sulaimán of the WBC (World Boxing Council) at a championship fight.

Me, with my precious daughter, Ava.

She's my blessing, my best friend.

Finding the right answer always starts with asking the right question.

— Jean Dancy

SIXTEEN

50 Questions

MARTY AND I were downstairs in Ali's office. We had been there about two hours when Veronica came in. She came and apologized very graciously for having to leave for the entire evening. About three hours later…

Marty: Muhammad, it's getting late. We'd better leave and come back another time.

Ali: No. Don't leave. Wait! Did you hear what your wife just said? I've gotta say something back. You've got to let me get her back, Marty.

Marty: (Laughing) Then she'll have something to say…and you'll have something to say…and we'll be here all night. I need to stop my wife right now. The later it gets…the more energy she gets. Trust me, she won't get tired.

Ali: (Laughing so hard he can barely talk) Marty, you've gotta let me tell her one more thing!

Marty: (To Ali) It's been another hour now. You and Jean haven't stopped. And you seem a little tired.

Ali: I've been sitting here since early this morning, I just need to lay down. Marty, you and Jean can come upstairs with me. That way I can lay on my bed and we can keep talking.

I can see Muhammad now. He kicked his shoes off, got on the bed and was lying on his back. Both hands behind his head and his legs crossed at the ankles. Though we had seen Ali's entire house, we had never spent time in Ali's bedroom before. I remember thinking, *I can't believe Marty and I are in Muhammad Ali's bedroom!*

Me: Oh Muhammad, I meant to share something with you. My teacher said that meeting you and having dinner at your house couldn't happen. She said it was an unrealistic expectation.

Ali: And now look at you…in the greatest bedroom in the world.

Me: She had me stand up and everything. I had written a paper saying that I would meet you and have dinner at your house.

Ali: You're just like me. We can stand at the top of a mountain…and see things that others can't see.

Me: Wait…Wait…Wait, Muhammad. I'm just like YOU?!! You really think I'm like You?!

Ali: Yes, you are. Are you here…with Muhammad Ali?

Me: What she said didn't bother me at all though. I knew we would meet, and I knew we'd be talking…just like this.

Ali: You knew it just like I knew I'd be champion of the world. I could always see it. People like your teacher don't have that. They go by what they see right in front of their eyes. They can't help it though. They just can't see what we see.

Me: Muhammad, I always knew that you and I were alike. I *knew* it! I knew that we would get to know each other. I used to say that a little chip inside of you would know the little chip inside of me. And now I'm here with you!

Ali: Do you know how many people…all over the world…millions and millions of people…want to meet me? I'm not being boastful either. That's just how it is. And out of all of those millions of people…all over the world, you're the one sitting here in my house. Sitting here talking with me.

Me: Wow!

Ali: People don't realize it…but it's all about what you believe. All about what you can see. Some people would have heard what your teacher said and forgot all about their dream. You're not like them. You're different. You're like me. Nobody can tell us that we don't see it. Nobody can keep us from getting it. I don't think all of those people are trying to be mean either. They just can't see what we see.

Marty: Ali, do you have any idea how many *more* questions my wife will ask you, if I don't take her home?

Ali: It's okay. She's got questions that nobody else ever asked me. I like her questions.

Marty and I were there for a very long time. The more Ali and I talked, the more we wanted to talk. Marty would have ended our conversation sooner but Ali and I had Marty laughing…to tears, at times.

Sometimes when people see themselves in you—their hearts are softer toward you.

— Jean Dancy

SEVENTEEN

The King's Heart

THE UNTHINKABLE HAPPENED one evening at Ali's house. And I thought that Marty and I would never be invited back.

Muhammad and Bundini were aware that Marty needed a manager and they were concerned and eager to help in any way that they could. Though Bundini knew, Ali was not aware that Marty had chosen a new manager.

Bundini had called earlier in the day saying, "Lil' Mamma, the Champ wants you and Marty to come over to the house tonight. I'll pick y'all up around seven." By then we were used to being invited to Ali's house; but it never lost its excitement.

Muhammad was like...not like Santa...but like a bigger than life kind of person...whose eyes twinkled like the stars to me. Being around him was not, by any stretch of the imagination, like being around a "regular person." He was wrapped in wonder and charisma and excitement. It was like he was covered in fairy-dust to me. He was purely magical.

After we had talked for just a few minutes, Muhammad wanted to know if Marty had found a new manager.

Ali: Marty, did you ever find a new manager?

Bundini: Champ, his wife is his manager.

Ali: All of our wives try to manage us. I mean a real manager…for his career.

Bundini: His wife is his manager.

Ali: Marty, did you ever find a new manager?

Bundini: (Speaking firmly) Champ! His *wife* is his new manager. They signed contracts and everything!

Ali: Marty, is that true?

Marty: Yes.

Ali: Jean, if Marty asked you to let him out of his contract and let a man manage him…would you let him out of it?

Me: Of course I would. I'll do whatever he wants me to do. He knows that.

Marty: (Very firmly) But I don't *want* her to let me out of it. I don't want a MAN to manage me.

Ali: Marty, you don't pick your wife to manage you just because she's pretty.

Marty: (Even firmer) I didn't choose her to manage me just because she's pretty.

Ali: She did a great deal for you at my office but boxing is a hard business. *Men* have trouble with it. How could you throw your wife out there...to swim with the sharks like that?

Marty: (Getting angry) I can throw my wife out there to swim with the sharks...because MY wife...knows how to swim with the sharks! If you knew my wife better when it comes to business you wouldn't be saying what you are saying.

Bundini: (Slowly) Marty...(As if to try to calm Marty down).

Marty: (Very angry) My WIFE is my manager...and that's THAT! Don't you run *your* business the way you want to? Well I run *my* business the way "I" want to.

Bundini: (Seeming nervous) Let's put some eggs in our shoes and beat it.

Bundini was standing and so was Marty. I was sitting there in *total* shock and disbelief. I was literally frozen in my seat. I seriously thought some wires would come down from the ceiling and hook themselves to my clothing and to Marty's and throw us out.

I knew Marty could be "street" and so raw…that's one of the things that I loved about him. That's what he would have told *any* other man…but my goodness…not MUHAMMAD ALI!!!

The wild horse had jumped the fence and I couldn't catch it. I could think only of the fact that I had *finally* met Ali. And that I was *finally* a guest in his home, welcome at his dinner table…and that Marty had messed it up! I wasn't upset with my husband though. I knew Marty Monroe. However, I wish I had had some kind of harness or stronger reins on his ultra masculine personality. I was usually able to calm things down before they went too far. But I didn't expect to be Marty's referee at Muhammad Ali's house!

I didn't even want to look at Ali's face. The room was silent…and I finally looked up to see Ali. I couldn't believe the expression on Ali's face and Bundini seemed equally surprised. Muhammad was smiling and looking at Marty like a proud big brother. Ali stood up.

Ali: A man is supposed to stand up for his beliefs. A man should stand up to ANYBODY who goes against what he believes. I respect that. And you're right. I run my business the way I want to run it. I don't back down from anybody when it comes to what I believe. And you should run your business the way *you* want to run it.

Then Ali went over to Marty flicking his left jab like lightening at Marty. Ali circled him like they were in the ring. Talking to Marty, trying to make him laugh, saying, "Show me what you got. C'mon, show me what you got. Show me what you got." After a while, that got to Marty and Marty started laughing and shadow boxing back with Muhammad.

Ali: (To Marty) Man, you're either real crazy or real brave.

Bundini: (Laughing) I think he's both, Champ.

Marty and Muhammad continued shadow boxing all over the room. I sat there thanking God that we had not been thrown out. Whew! The rest of the evening felt like whipped cream on my favorite cake.

If Muhammad had been even *slightly* insecure as a man, he wouldn't have reacted to Marty the way he did. He couldn't have. Muhammad had every advantage. After all, he was Muhammad Ali and we were in *his* house. My admiration for Muhammad went...up, up, up... even higher.

Ali seemed amused and pleased by Marty's firm stance on his beliefs. The four of us laughed and talked a few more hours. When we were leaving Ali surprised me again.

Ali: (With excitement in his voice and wide eyes) Bundini, bring them back tomorrow night!

Ali seemed invigorated by what happened that night. I got a chance to see Ali, the man, the human being, who was able to see Marty's right to Marty's beliefs. Muhammad had stood up so heroically in public for what he believed. And he had shown us in private that he

139

was no hypocrite. Ali not only admired Marty for the position that Marty took on his beliefs, but Ali fully understood Marty's right to take that position.

On the way home…

Bundini: Marty, the Champ gets tired of "yes men." I get tired of them too. Everybody's so busy trying to be around the Champ… they forget who they are. You and Lil' Mamma are not like that. Y'all a breath of fresh air to the Champ. People so busy draining the Champ. They all want something from him. You and Lil' Mamma give the Champ something.

Muhammad Ali didn't have one rule for himself and a different rule for another man. Ali was a real man. And he appreciated being in the presence of another *real* man. Ali truly had the heart of a king.

With faith...we can reach the sky
without a ladder.
— Jean Dancy

EIGHTEEN

The Invitation

ONE DAY I called Muhammad just to say "Hello," and he asked if Marty and I could come over immediately. By that time, Marty and I had begun to visit him regularly. Sometimes we'd be called by Bundini who would say, "The Champ wants to see you and Marty at the house this evening." My heart would always flutter just a little when we were on our way to Ali's house. Marty would lean over and kiss me on the forehead, as if he instinctively knew. I never took those visits for granted. A big beautiful red Christmas bow was always on them.

To the person on the phone Ali said, "I've got to go. I'm about to have a very important meeting."

Ali: (To Me) What have you done about getting ready for Marty's next fight?

Me: I've hired a cook, some sparring partners, and I'm setting up a camp near Palm Springs.

Ali: I called you and Marty over here because I want y'all to be a part of my camp. It'll be good for the boxers to have somebody like you to talk to. I hear they have all kind of problems…and I hear you can help them.

Me: Help them how?

Ali: Some of them have management problems. They can't afford lawyers and they need somebody to explain contracts to them. Boxers have all kinds of problems. They may just need somebody to talk to sometimes. Bundini says you're a boxer's best friend. He wants you and Marty there too.

Me: Wow, Muhammad, I don't even have to think about my answer. I love helping boxers. But I have to check with my husband. (Looking at Marty, smiling) It's whatever he says.

Ali: And Marty, we can train together and help each other out. Run, chop wood…everything.

Marty: Whatever my wife wants to do is fine with me. She's the one setting up everything.

Me: What will I do about the people I've already hired? And trainer, Bill Slayton, is with us now too.

Ali: Bring everybody with you if you want to. I already have a cook in my camp, Lana. But you can eat at a restaurant everyday if you want to. You and all of the people you decide to bring with you. I will pay for everything. I'll reimburse you for all of the money you've already spent and for any money you spend after you leave. If you feel you need to pay somebody that you're not bringing with you to Deer Lake, I'll pay for that too.

Me: Gosh, that's so nice of you.

Ali: This is business. You're doing me a favor. The least I can do is cover your expenses. I know Marty's not hired to be my sparring partner. He's got his own sparring partners. But he'll be paid every week. And you'll be paid too.

Me: Muhammad, I've already been given expense money to set up my own camp. You don't have to reimburse me for anything. We'll need airfare though, that's all.

Ali: I insist on covering everything. Airfare and everything. And when we leave my camp and travel, all of that will be covered too. (Smiling at me) Manager, I need you to keep a record of every penny you spend out of your pocket. Even the tips at the airport. You wouldn't even be flying if I hadn't invited you to be in Deer Lake. I don't care who else is paying you. Muhammad Ali is paying you too.

Me: I feel so honored that you would ask us to be there. And Muhammad, I *love* helping boxers, reading contracts for them, and giving them advice.

Ali: And don't go around asking the people who work for me what you're supposed to be doing. They don't know. If you have any questions when you get there, come to me.

Marty and I took six other people with us to Deer Lake: Trainer, Bill Slayton; Marty's brother, Mac; Marty's assistant; and three sparring partners.

Knowledge has no gender.

—— Jean Dancy

NINETEEN

Deer Lake Camp

THE AIR WAS electric with excitement! Like firecrackers sizzling in the background…just waiting to take to the sky when Ali appeared. People from all over the world anticipated Ali like children looking for Santa on Christmas morning.

A rainbow color of people covered the camp like a carpet. We could hear people talking as we walked through, "I just wanna see his face." Others were more insistent, "I've got to shake his hand. I came all the way from Egypt just to shake his hand."

I tried to take it all in and process what I was seeing. It was like nothing I had ever seen or heard of before. It was as if people thought by touching Ali something magical would happen to them. Like Ali would touch them and they would at *least* be able to fly! Seriously. They didn't need to be his friend, like me. They just needed a touch from him, one touch…anything. People from all over the world waited, trying to see him.

When people saw that we were affiliated with Ali, we were treated like…we were affiliated with Ali. They had questions for us. They sent messages to Ali. They took pictures with us and wanted autographs. Though Marty and I had experienced people wanting pictures with us and autographs before, everything was bumped up to "times ten" in Ali's camp.

The camp is located high atop a hill. The view below from certain angles is absolutely breath-taking, especially at night. Being there felt like going back in time. Like we had gone to the Little House on the Prairie. The camp is made of log cabins and we even pumped fresh water from a well. Bundini had talked about the well water there like it flowed straight from heaven. And it really was amazingly refreshing and delicious. There were huge rocks with the names of legendary boxers on them.

On the right side of camp there were two gorgeous little ponies for Ali's children, Hana and Laila. Hana and Laila were icing on the cake for me. I adored those little girls and I spent as much time with them as I could.

There were bodyguards standing outside of Ali's cabin armed and ready to do whatever was necessary to protect Ali; although I've never seen anyone more loved. People were sometimes tearful as they expressed their love for him.

The boxing gym wasn't that big so it was standing room only for most people. The highlight of the day was the chance to see Ali in the ring sparring. He was the ring master...and it was his circus. We were his willing audience and he dazzled us and dangled us almost over the cliff of excitement but he brought us back. Just as we came down from his lightening fast jab, he'd take us right back up again with the "Ali shuffle!" Oh, how I thanked God for allowing me to be there, for allowing us to be there.

I was mesmerized by the sight of my husband. He took my breath away if he appeared before I expected to see him. I would turn my head talking with people, turn back...and voila...Marty would be in the ring loosening up. Adrenaline would rush through my veins like a roller coaster ride; and Ali (laughing) would often see my face and point to Marty.

Watching Marty spar was one of the most exciting things I have ever seen. And watching him spar with Ali was more exciting than the Super Bowl and The Playoffs happening at the same time. I was in boxing heaven people!!!

When training was over people from all over the world waited trying to see Ali close-up and touch him. The atmosphere was much like that of a carnival. People were selling t-shirts, pictures, and other Ali memorabilia.

When Ali came out, like the parting of the Red Sea, people automatically shifted from where they were—to where Ali was. It was a sight to see.

Reporters who had interviewed Ali were asking to see the "female boxing manager." They inquired about me like I was the lady who had just arrived from Mars.

Reporter: Hello, are you the female boxing manager?

Me: Yes, I am.

Reporter: Is it difficult being a *female* boxing manager?

Me: I think being a boxing manager can be difficult for anyone.

Reporter: Is it more difficult for you because you're a woman?

Me: Yes, it is. It's at least three times more difficult for me.

Reporter: What advice would you give a woman who wants to be a boxing manager?

Me: (Laughing) Run...run to the hills! No, seriously...I would tell her to first be in love with boxing. Don't do it for the money. And do your homework. Know at least three times more than you need to know. Knowledge is power. *Knowledge has no gender.*

Marty and I never minded giving interviews. And both of us felt that being in Muhammad Ali's Deer Lake Camp was far more interesting and exciting than we could have ever imagined.

I particularly enjoyed helping boxers and being there for them; and it was always surprising when they wanted me to manage them.

Love is the most expensive gift that you will ever give.

— Jean Dancy

TWENTY

Breakfast with the King

A **FEW DAYS** after being at Deer Lake, Ali invited me to have breakfast with him. We sat across from each other at the table in the kitchen. We were alone except for Lana, Ali's cook, bringing things back and forth to the table. Ali was quite animated. With wide eyes and a big, big smile on his face, he made an announcement:

Ali: Jean…you have hit the big time! You are the ONLY female boxing manager…in the biggest boxing camp in the W-O-R-L-D!!! You are here with Muhammad Aleeeee!!!

I'd never thought of it that way. What a way to start our breakfast. Conversation flowed so easily. He invited me back to breakfast the next day.

When I arrived the next day, however, it was standing room only. There were cameras everywhere and reporters from all over the world! I thought, of course—immediately—that Ali had forgotten that he invited me to have breakfast with him. He had not.

Ali was the same as he had been the day before. Then it hit me…that Ali lives in a fishbowl and the world is always watching him. After awhile, the reporters started asking Ali questions. It was amazingly comfortable to me.

Then pretty little, Hana Ali, marched around the corner and sat in Muhammad's lap. I can see her now. She placed her little arm around her dad's neck and looked around the room as if to say, *This is my dad, my Muhammad Ali. He belongs to meee!*

Of course everybody laughed and thought it was cute. But you could tell that the reporters thought Ali would ask her to leave so he could continue answering questions. He did not. Instead, he stopped the interview and placed big big kisses on Hana's face. His actions showed her that the sun rose and sat on her, that as his child, she was the center of his universe. He was so loving and so affectionate to her. It warmed my heart almost to tears. Such a beautiful sight to see. You could actually *feel* their love for each other.

I clearly remember the shoes that she wore that day. Beautiful black patent leather shoes fit for a little princess. I couldn't help wondering if those were the shoes that Jenita, her nanny, had laid out for her— or if Hana (such a strong little girl!) had insisted on wearing those shoes herself.

Hana sat on her dad's lap and gazed at everybody like *she* had called a meeting. After she had soaked in her dad's love like a little sponge, she jumped down and left as quickly as she arrived.

That moment stands out in my mind like a beautiful rose because of the love that I saw and felt him extend to her. She seemed to have been about four years old at the time.

I adored Ali's little girls. And sometimes I carried Laila on my hip. Hana was often much too busy to stay with Laila and me very long. Laila was about a year younger than Hana.

It's okay to wear pink into the boardroom.

— Jean Dancy

TWENTY-ONE

Ali and Women's Rights

~~~◦~~~

MARTY DECIDED TO take a few boxers out to dinner with us, including our dearest friend, Jeff "Showtime" Stoudemire. Showtime was one of the best, most exciting boxers in Ali's camp and a great friend. We went to a restaurant down the hill close to Ali's camp. I will always remember that night…and never forget it because they had the best chocolate cheesecake ever. Actually, that was the first time I ever had any chocolate cheesecake. Delicious… delicious. What an introduction. I had two slices!

All of the food was delicious but the waitress was a thorn in our sides. She left an unpleasant taste in my mouth. Near the end of the evening, and it was a long evening, she turned from vinegar to honey just in time to get a good tip. Marty always gave very generous tips even if he only ordered a cup of coffee. However, she tried to play us like we were virgin violins. That didn't sit well with me at all. Since he left the choice to me, I stopped Marty from leaving a tip.

The following day Marty and I were standing in the center of Deer Lake Camp. We were surrounded by people from all over the world. A man who worked for Ali approached Marty. I will call him "Bruce." His body language was aggressive, disrespectful, and rude.

Bruce: (Talking to Marty, his voice elevated) I heard you ate at the restaurant last night and you didn't leave a tip. You're a part of this camp now. And you made the whole camp look bad!

I saw my husband's body language. He could go from 0-100 very quickly…with no stops in between if he felt disrespected. It was even too late for me to smoothly intervene.

My husband was a tall, gorgeous, gentle…lion. However, his smooth, quiet, calm, polished demeanor caused some people to mistake him for another kind of animal. Though Marty and I had become Born-again Christians, Jesus was still working on Marty's temper.

The nicer gist of what he said is as follows…

Marty: First of all…don't you EVER come in my face like this again! Man, you don't tell me what to do or when to do it. I tip when I get ready. You said I made the whole camp look bad, how are you making the camp look right now?

My husband's voice could sound so cold and threatening. Marty stepped to him like they were in the ring—face-to-face, almost nose to nose. You would have thought that the referee was about to give the boxing instructions.

The man slinked back—in shock! And in fear it seemed. I'm sure he didn't expect that from Marty. He looked like he had walked into the lion's den accidentally. And he was trying to slowly back out of it without being seen.

It was too late. All eyes were on them. All conversation stopped. Marty was talking to Bruce and Marty was hitting his own chest with his hands. That was never good. The man actually took a few more steps back and quickly scurried away like a squirrel.

My husband was polite and respectful to everyone, all the time. However, he would not allow anyone to disrespect him. And he would become a volcano—if he even *thought* someone was trying to disrespect me!

I took Marty's hand and tried to soothe his anger away. A gentle touch from me always worked at those times. I was grateful that Marty was rarely angry to that degree with people—and my husband was *never* like that with me. Ever! The crowd seemed to take a collective deep breath…and a sigh of relief.

The following day Bruce saw me alone.

Bruce: Jean, you really have your hands full with Marty.

Me: Why would you say that?

Bruce: I hope you never make him mad.

Me: Bruce, I am quite sure that no wife on planet Earth is treated better than my husband treats me—everyday. I have a wonderful husband and he adores me. We adore each other. I don't have any problems with Marty.

Bruce seemed annoyed by my statement and totally agitated. It was as if he wanted me to be angry with Marty also.

Bruce: When the camp goes to New York next week, you won't be going with Marty. You'll go to New York a few days later when the wives and women go.

Me: But I'm not just Marty's wife, I'm also his manager. The other boxers will have their managers with them, won't they?

Bruce: I'm just telling you that you won't be there until later.

Me: But I take care of Marty's business.

Bruce: Then I don't know what to tell you. The women are coming later. And that's that. I guess Marty will have to take care of his own business.

I knew that was Bruce's way of getting back at Marty in a very passive aggressive way. I was so glad Marty hadn't heard him. Whew!

Me: Darling, Bruce just told me that I can't go to New York next week when you and Ali and the men go.

Marty: If you don't go, I'm not going either.

Me: Marty, you can't just NOT go. You're doing an exhibition with Muhammad Ali at *Madison Square Garden*! You *have* to go!

Marty: I'm not gonna let anybody disrespect you…as a woman, or as my manager. I see what that man is trying to do. And I won't allow it. Go tell Ali that if you can't go when we go, then I won't go either!

Me: Darling, I will take care of this. You know I will.

I had no intention, absolutely *no* intention of going to Ali telling him what Marty said. I would handle it…but *my* way. I felt that my job as a manager was to diffuse potentially explosive situations. I wasn't going to take a problem to Ali. I had one objective and that objective was to go with Ali and Marty when they left for New York. I knew that objective could be achieved with a kinder…gentler approach. As a boxing manager, I was always throwing water on firecrackers.

I went straight to the outside of Ali's cabin. An armed security guard was always outside. I never went to Ali for anything but I talked with him all the time. I would walk outside of Ali's cabin and say: Hello, Ali. I'm just walking by. He always said, "Come on in. Don't just walk by." So that's what I did that day and he invited me in.

I went in and he seemed delighted to see me. His smile was always as radiant as the sun to me. Seeing him was like having an audience with the king. Literally. People in the camp couldn't just go prancing in there and see Ali at will. Every time I was in Ali's cabin, he had personally invited me in. We laughed and talked for about 30 minutes before I mentioned New York.

Me: Ali, I hope you won't need me for anything in New York when Marty does the exhibition with you, because I was told that I won't be going when you and Marty go.

Ali: Why?

Me: I don't know. I was just told that I can't go when the men go. He said I will go later when the wives and women go.

Ali: What?! Who told you that? That didn't come from *me*.

Me: Bruce told me that.

Ali: When did he tell you that?

Me: Yesterday.

Ali was visibly unhappy about that.

Ali: (In a controlled tone) Jean, you have my word that this will *never* happen again. I will speak with him today, *myself.*

Me: Thank you! Thank you so much!

Ali: I promise you it will never happen again. You are not just here as Marty's wife, you are also here as his manager. A woman doing business here. The only female boxing manager here. And I will not allow anyone to disrespect you...in any way. I'm proud of you. Proud of what you do.

Me: Ali, thank you so much. That's so kind of you.

Ali: No. That's what's right. I'm not gonna have you here...in my camp...treated like some second-class citizen...just because you're a woman. From now on...you and Marty go everywhere I go. And if anybody's got a problem with it....this is MY camp. I invited you and Marty here. *Nobody* can have a problem with that.

I had to actually fight tears as he talked. Ali was my big brave hero. The more I was around him, the greater he became. He was the greatest—as a person—period. His heart was bigger than the moon and brighter than the sun.

Every time I was in his presence, he praised me, the way Marty and my mother did. I always left him feeling happier and even better about myself than I had felt before seeing him.

Bruce saw me again and tucked his tail like he had lost his bark. He had *clearly* been dealt with by Ali.

Muhammad Ali rolled out the red carpet for me in boxing—when some men were trying to pull it from under my feet—and make me fall. He stood up for me and my rights as a woman. Yes, Muhammad Ali was all about women's rights.

No matter what life serves you, just don't forget the cake.
— Jean Dancy

TWENTY-TWO

Happy Birthday!

ONE SPARKLING NIGHT in Beverly Hills the stars came out for Ali's private birthday party. It was his 50th birthday. I arrived with Tommy Hearns in a lovely Rolls Royce. A magical, fairy-tale feeling was in the air.

The party was at Chasen's restaurant, a favorite for celebrities like Sammy Davis Jr. and Frank Sinatra. For starters, Tommy Hearns is one of my all-time favorite boxers and one of my favorite people on earth. A dear friend. He is such a gentleman; and I could feel him walking on cotton with me. He didn't want to say or do anything that might seem insensitive since it was my first time going out to an event without Marty. It had only been a few months since my darling husband went to heaven—a sudden heart attack.

Immediately after we walked inside, Ken Norton rushed over to me and said, "Hi Jean, where's Marty?" The words just fell out of his mouth. My husband and I had been inseparable so I understood. Then Ken paused, apologized for having said that, and hugged me so tenderly. I fought tears.

Tommy and I took a few more steps and I saw a line of people trying to personally greet Muhammad. Ali stood in the center of the room like royalty. Though we had talked on the phone, we had not seen each other in person for a few years.

So much had happened. The king of the ring (Ali, himself) had retired. I had become a boxing promoter. Marty's promoter. My darling, my precious husband, had moved to heaven. Muhammad and Veronica were no longer married; and his new wife, Lonnie, was there.

I couldn't help wondering if the illness that affected Ali would keep him from recognizing me right away. Ali turned his head slightly and his eyes hugged me before his arms did. He opened his arms for me and it felt like time stood still. The twinkle in his eyes gave way to compassion. Ali hugged me and looked me in the eyes like he didn't know what to say. Then he spoke, still hugging me.

Ali: This is the first time I've ever seen you out...without Marty.

Me: (Fighting the feeling that comes just before tears) I know.

Ali: I love you.

Me: I love you too.

Ali: I love you…I love you…I love you.

I felt that I could face everybody else after facing him. Without question, Ali felt like family to me. Like Marty, he was my brave hero, my precious friend.

People started coming up giving me such wonderful compliments. The following things were said:

I always admired you and Marty.

Everybody could see that you and Marty adored each other.

I always thought you were an attorney. The way you handled business. Your knowledge about boxing always shocked people.

You spoke so articulately on TV.

You and Marty did things in boxing that have never been done before.

One man there, a legend in the boxing business, had more compliments for me than anyone else. Finally I asked him why he had never told me any of those things before. Laughing, he said, "I wasn't about to say any of those things to Marty Monroe's wife!" However, he could have said all of those things. Marty wouldn't have had any problem with that because all of those things were very nice and very respectful.

Those compliments (particularly that night), bathed me and hugged me. They also lifted me; and made me feel that I was appreciated for having been Marty's manager and promoter.

Ali looked across the room and smiled at me. I smiled at him. He sent a wide-eyed playful smile back. It felt like he was checking on me.

I got a chance to spend some more time with Ken Norton before he left the party. He told me all about his motorcycle accident. Said the doctors told him he would never walk again.

Me: Ken, how did you feel when they told you that you'd never walk again?

Ken: I didn't pay any attention to that. I knew I would get out of that bed and walk again.

He gave me a big bear hug before he left. Ken's comment reminded me of the sheer courage and strength that I had seen close up in my husband, in Ali, Joe Frazier, Tommy Hearns, and in Ken. I'm convinced that God uses a different kind of recipe for certain boxers, for certain men.

The night became increasingly more comforting to me. It was so nice to see Ali's daughters, Hana and Laila again; Gene Kilroy (Ali's business representative); and Sugar Ray Robinson's lovely, sweet, wife.

Some of the most successful people in Hollywood, sports, and in the entertainment industry, were at Ali's party. However, when

Muhammad Ali was in a room, he was the king...the *only* king. And everybody wanted an audience with him. I didn't blame them. That's why I was particularly grateful that I got an opportunity to talk with him again. The atmosphere between us was lighter then and we were able to laugh a little, take pictures, and talk.

One of my biggest dreams came true that night. I always wanted to be in the presence of Tommy Hearns and Ali—at the same time. And there I was—with Muhammad Ali on one side of me—and Tommy Hearns on the other side. I felt so loved and protected. Lots of pictures were taken of Ali, Tommy, and me together. Oh, how I treasure those pictures.

In spite of everything, God allowed me to have a warm wonderful... magical night. One of the best nights of my life. Thanks, God.

God can put you at the front of the longest line.

— Jean Dancy

TWENTY-THREE

Book Soup

AVA: MOM, I don't think it's fair for me to go with you to your friend's book signing…if you won't go with me to hear my voice teacher sing tonight.

Me: Darling, my friend's book signing is only for one night. And your voice teacher is singing tomorrow night as well.

Ava: Couldn't we just go by the Book Soup first. You could say, "Hello" to him and we could still go hear my teacher sing?

Me: Darling, no…we can't because there will be so many people there. And he's expecting us to be there the whole night.

As a child, Ava couldn't quite grasp the magnitude of an event involving *my* friend.

I hadn't seen a line that long since I went to the Apollo theater to see James Brown! I gave my word that I would be there for Muhammad Ali's book signing. Muhammad didn't know what time he would arrive. I didn't know what time we would arrive. However, just as my footsteps and Ava's were about to reach the entrance of the Book Soup bookstore, I saw Muhammad getting out of a car. Amazing!

Muhammad got out of the car, gave us wide eyes and that big gorgeous smile. He hugged us. Then he put one arm around Ava and one arm around me and walked with us inside. It was wonderful to say the least. Howard Bingham, Ali's photographer, followed closely behind us.

There were actually celebrities in line. One of the first faces I saw was a legendary male singer. Some people had seen us enter with Muhammad. I was wearing a black baseball cap with red boxing gloves on it and people were trying to get me—to get them—to Ali. I did help the singer get to Ali more quickly though.

Later, Ali's daughter, Hana, and one of her friends arrived and we were all in the back talking with Ali as people waited to get inside.

Ali touched Ava's face and said, "Girl, you look just like your daddy!" At that moment a picture was taken of Ali and Ava that we cherish.

I watched Ali sign books for hours…and hours. His hands were cramping but he would not stop signing those books. The Book

Soup had to close the doors at a certain time. I've never seen a more generous celebrity with his fans and with his time.

Ali is thought of as the greatest boxer—but he was the greatest at everything that I ever saw him do. The same magic about Ali that captured me as a little girl, is the same magic that intrigued me as a grown woman. It wasn't a figment of my childhood imagination—it was real. The magic was real! And it excites me…still.

Conversations With Muhammad Ali

I had conversations in my head with Muhammad Ali l-o-n-g before I ever met him. Then we met—and I had actual conversations with him.

I searched through my journals and my mind, trying to decide which ones to share with you. I chose the following ones because I think they are representative of Ali's heart, his personality, and his philosophy of life.

Hated Joe Frazier! I've never hated Joe Frazier. I've never even disliked him. In fact, I love Joe Frazier.

Conversation 1

Me: But I used to think you hated Joe Frazier.

Ali: Hated Joe Frazier! I've never hated Joe Frazier. I've never even disliked him. In fact, I love Joe Frazier.

Me: I bet people would be so surprised to know that you love Joe.

Ali: If I could have Joe Frazier as my best friend, I would.

Me: If it hadn't been for you, I wouldn't have ever liked him. I made a decision a long time ago to dislike the people that you dislike.

Ali: Jean, I was saying all those things about Joe Frazier just to sell tickets. I didn't mean any of that stuff! I probably took it too far... but I just wanted all the tickets to sell. I didn't want to let Joe down after giving me that chance to fight him. I did it for Joe...and for myself.

Me: Did you know that Joe was Marty's manager before I became Marty's manager?

Ali: No, I didn't know that. (Laughing, joking) You mean you replaced *Joe Frazier?* Is he coming up here looking for you? Do I need to hide?

Me: Muhammad, because Joe was Marty's manager, I've spent a lot of time around him. He is one of the most beautiful men I have ever met. Just like you said. So much fun and so generous. I loved hanging out with him.

Ali: See, you would have missed out on all of that just because of me.

Me: But that's how much I love you, Muhammad.

Ali: If I do wrong...will you take my side?

Me: No. I would never do that. Why would you ask me something like that?

Ali: I'm glad you said that. Never do wrong just because you love somebody. And never hate anybody.

Me: I didn't *hate* Joe. I just wouldn't have been open to being his friend if you hadn't told me how much you love him.

Ali: But that's my point, you would have missed out on one of the best men in the world. I don't dislike any of my opponents and I don't hate anybody. Especially not Joe Frazier. He brings out the best in me.

Me: I don't hate anybody either.

Ali: People say I hate white people but I don't. Sometimes people think you hate them because they hate you. But if I hated white people, would Gene Kilroy be up here? I run this camp. Nobody can be here if I don't want them here.

The world never saw me in my prime. I never saw myself in my prime.

Conversation 2

Ali: People always want to compare great boxers to Muhammad Ali.

Me: But can you blame them?

Ali: Yes, I can blame them…because the world never saw me in my prime. I never saw myself in my prime.

Me: Muhammad, I never thought about that.

Ali: Well think about it. If you take the fastest man on earth… running. Break both of his legs, bones all messed up. Make him sit down for over three years. OVER THREE YEARS! Then ask him to come run against younger runners. They've been active. Never stopped running. And just because his legs are not broken anymore…he's supposed to take up where he left off. (Eyes wide) Would that seem fair to you?

Me: That wouldn't seem fair at all. But Muhammad, what if the runner who didn't run for over three years looks like he's not only on the same level as all of the younger active runners…but he's even better than they are?

Ali: EXACTLY! I'm being compared to boxers who should run circles around me in the ring. But they can't. If I'm this great now, if I'm this fast now, what would I look like in the ring if those years hadn't been taken away from me?!

Me: Wow!

Ali: And I'm still this fast? And I'm still this accurate? A heavyweight. Not a welterweight. Not a flyweight. I'm not trying to take anything away from anybody else either. I just want my critics to be fair. No other boxer can be compared to Muhammad Ali…because no other boxer has turned down millions of dollars and had over three years taken from him. I didn't walk away. Those years were taken away from me because of my beliefs. No other boxer came back and was better than the boxers who never left. I'm the ONLY boxer who ever did that.

Me: So that means you're even greater than the greatest?

Ali: (Laughing) Is that how you see it?

Me: Yes, that's how I see it.

Ali: (Very seriously) Don't get me wrong. I'm not complaining. If I had it to do over…I'd do the same thing. Stand up for what I believe.

Me: Muhammad, you are so amazing.

Ali: Most people have money as their God. Not truth. Not honor. Not their beliefs.

Me: That's true.

Ali: Threaten to take their money away…and their beliefs change fast. Real men stand up for what they believe. Real *people* stand up for what they believe.

Me: My mother says that you and your word are one. If your word is no good—you are no good. And she says that you *are* what you believe.

Ali: And she's right. Your mother is right. We don't have to wait to see if a person will go before a firing-squad or not. It comes out in little things…all the time.

Ernie Shavers hits harder than anybody whoever hit me.

Conversation 3

Me: Hi Muhammad, I just called to ask you a question.

Ali: What are you and Marty doing?

Me: We just left the gym. I'm calling from the car.

Ali: Y'all come over here. Come over here and ask your question…I know you've got more than one question.

Me: But Muhammad, I need you to answer this question right now. I've already decided what I'm going to do, but I want your opinion on this. You should have seen the men at the gym today…trying to make me take a fight. Especially Bundini. He's been calling me non-stop but I need to know what you think.

Ali: What fight?

Me: One with Ernie Shavers. His opponent fell out and they want to replace the opponent with Marty.

Ali: Ernie Shavers?

Me: Yes. What do you think?

Ali: Marty's a lot younger than Ernie Shavers. He's taller, faster, and Marty can box. You know that styles make fights. Marty's got the style to beat Ernie.

Me: So are you saying I should take the fight too like Bundini and all of the men at the gym are saying? Marty's had back problems and he hasn't been able to run or train properly.

Ali: When is the fight?

Me: He'd have less than two weeks to get ready and it's a TV fight.

Ali: You always want to be ready for a fight.

Me: I know.

Ali: And just so you know, Ernie Shavers hits harder that anybody whoever hit me.

Me: Whaaat?! Harder than Foreman? Harder than...

Ali: (Interrupting) Harder than George Foreman. Harder than anybody who's ever hit me.

Me: I wasn't going to take the fight anyway because Marty hasn't had enough time to train. But for sure I'm not going to take it now... (laughing) after what you said! Are you going to be home all evening?

Ali: Where else would I be?

Me: You're Muhammad Ali, you could be anywhere in the world this evening! I'll call you back if we're not coming over.

Ali: Call me back anyway...and put Marty on the phone.

Me: Okay.

No matter who you are…you're going
to be hit.
You're going to be tested.

Conversation 4

Ali: Before you ask, I already know what you wanna know.

Me: (Smiling) You may know many things but you do not… necessarily…know what I want to know today. Okay, what do I want to know?

Ali: You want to know why the sparring went the way it did today. You want to know why I barely used my jab at all with Marty today. You want to know why I changed my style with Marty today.

Me: Well Muhammad…I want to know why the sparring went the way it did today. I want to know why you barely used your jab at all with Marty today. I want to know why you changed your style with Marty today.

We laughed so hard!

Ali: What did I tell you? Sparring was different today. And I knew you would want to know exactly why.

Me: Well?

Ali: Marty's going in there with Eddie "The Animal" Lopez. It could be a war. The Animal's never been stopped. Marty's never been stopped. Never been knocked down. Never been knocked out. This fight won't go the distance. Somebody's gonna be stopped.

Me: Somebody?!

Ali: I'm just messing with you. Marty can box him *or* go toe-to-toe. The Animal won't be boxing. He's gonna try to put pressure on Marty. Try to smother all his punches. Try to keep him out the center of the ring. Take him to the ropes.

Me: If he takes Marty to the ropes, Marty's going to surprise him with some combinations. I never worry about Marty on the ropes.

Ali: The best way I can help Marty get ready for this fight…is to do what I did today.

Me: It looked more like a real fight to me than sparring.

Ali: It just *looked* like that. Marty's not a gym fighter…I'm not a gym fighter. What you saw today was child's play. Nobody got hurt.

Me: It was so exciting though! Oh my gosh!!

Ali: What did you think of Marty?

Me: I was pleased, particularly when he was on the ropes. I love his combinations from the ropes. The better question is…what did *you* think of Marty today? Do you think he's ready? The fight is pretty soon.

Ali: He's where he needs to be. I'm gonna make a prediction. The fight won't go the distance.

Me: I hope not. I'll be glad when it's over.

Ali: Marty's tall…like me. Not a real big heavyweight. He's already down to 210 lbs. But he's got a powerful right hand. And it's accurate. He can hurt you with either hand. When Marty lands that first big right hand he's gonna daze the animal. Hit him with combinations. Another right hand…and it'll be all over.

Me: How far do you see the fight going?

Ali: Marty will stop him in the first half of the fight. It won't even go six rounds. Unless Marty keeps that jab in his face…it's gonna be a war though. Marty's chin is a gift. He's got lead in it. You can't give that to yourself. My chin is a gift. No matter how hard you train, either you have a good chin…or you don't. Marty can give it and Marty can take it.

Me: But I don't want him to take it.

Ali: No boxer should go out there trying to prove he can take a punch. That's crazy! But sooner or later…no matter who you are…if you're matched right, and if you're in there with world-class opponents… you're going to get hit. You're going to be tested.

*Marty stopped Eddie "The Animal" Lopez in round five. And it was a war!

We don't know the strength of a man who has never been down. Never been tested.

Conversation 5

Me: (On the phone) Hi Muhammad…

Ali: What's wrong?

Me: Everything that could go wrong went wrong in the fight with Page. For starters, Marty couldn't run for two weeks because of his back. He was in so much pain in his dressing room—BEFORE the fight! He had a cold. But he fought anyway.

Ali: So why are you so upset? Boxers are like that. We go to war when we know we're already hurt. That's what we do.

Me: I'm upset because people don't know that he could barely walk…couldn't even loosen up in the dressing room. I don't want people to think that Marty was at his best and couldn't do any better than that.

Ali: You can't control what people think.

Me: After the fight even Greg Page *himself* wondered what was wrong with Marty.

Ali: These things happen. The fight is over and you just have to move on.

Me: But it hurts. Really hurts.

Ali: The key is doing your best in any situation.

Me: I'm grateful that Marty didn't get knocked down or knocked out but…

Ali: People who know Marty…know something was wrong. They didn't see the fire or energy that he brings to the ring. You can't look at Marty's fight with Lynn Ball and look at his fight with Page and *not* know that something was wrong.

Me: If I could, I would get a loud speaker and tell everybody what happened.

Ali: You're gonna learn that people think what they want to think. Some people thought I was afraid to go to war for my country; and nothing could have been further from the truth. What people think or what people see, depends on the people—not on truth.

Me: Muhammad, when I went to pick up our money, the men in the room stopped talking. They looked at me like they thought I was going to cry. I would have slapped a tear back in my eye before I would have allowed them to see me cry.

Ali: (Laughing) You won't let 'em see you sweat?!

Me: Never!

Ali: (Laughing) Woman you're something else. Where's Marty?

Me: He went to the gym.

Ali: Call me when he gets back and put him on the phone. A real man knows how to win and lose with the same strength. I don't mean just boxing either. I mean in life. Marty will be okay.

Me: When you lost to Joe Frazier, I thought it would break you in some way.

Ali: A lot of people thought that. A strong man keeps getting up and keeps going on after he faces adversity. We don't know the strength of a man who's never been down. Never been tested.

But wouldn't you rather be out there
shopping…and buying pretty dresses…and
all the pretty things that ladies buy?

Conversation 6

Ali: Jean…You have hit the big time!

Me: Whaat?! What did I do to hit the big time?

Ali: You're the *only* female boxing manager…in the biggest boxing camp in the W-O-R-L-D! You're here with Muhammad Aleeeee!

Me: (Laughing) I never thought about it like that. Thanks for pointing that out to me. Muhammad, you're always lifting me and praising me…the way my mother and Marty always do. I really appreciate that.

Ali: Where are the other female boxing managers up here? Where are they?

Me: Oh Muhammad, you're far more beautiful in person than I ever imagined you would be.

Ali: Did you talk with the reporters yesterday?

Me: Muhammad, you should have *seen* them! They were walking around saying, "Where's the female boxing manager?" Like I was from another planet or something.

Muhammad: Being here is much bigger than being from another planet. Did they interview you?

Me: Yes. I did about six interviews. They took pictures and everything. How did they even know I was here? Did you tell them?

Ali: The whole world needs to know you're here. I've never seen a woman like you. The women go shopping…and you wanna hang out with Marty and me and Bundini. Why is that?

Me: Do we have fun…laughing and talking about boxing…the four of us? Nobody would ever guess how funny you are.

Ali: But wouldn't you rather be out there shopping…and buying pretty dresses…and all the pretty things that ladies buy?

Me: Actually, no. I'd rather be with Marty and you and Bundini.

Ali: Bundini says I need to see the other side of you. He says in a business meeting in Minnesota, the pit bull came out.

Me: (Laughing) Whaat?!

Ali: Before you get upset, he says you're always nice and professional…but nobody can walk over you. He says you never get loud or use bad words.

Me: He's right. And like I always say, raising your voice doesn't raise your point. I'm never loud or rude. I don't use bad words. I never resort to that kind of behavior in business. For me, it's not necessary. But I can be very, *very* firm...and that tends to surprise people at times.

Ali: Guess what Marty said about you?

Me: What? What did he say?

Ali: Marty said, "My wife is sweet, but maaaan, my wife cracks a mean whip!"

Me: (Laughing) I know he said it. I know he said it…because he says it all the time!

It's just one king. And millions of people.
Sometimes the king has to be protected from
all of the people pulling at him.

Conversation 7

Me: Muhammad, a man grabbed me yesterday...almost by the ankles...begging me to give you a message from him.

Ali: Who is the man? Do I know him? And what is the message?

Me: You don't know the man. He says he came from the other side of the world...just to shake your hand. That's his biggest dream in life...just to touch you and shake your hand.

Ali: Okay.

Me: But yesterday when you finished training, there were so many people around you, he said that just as he reached for your hand, one of your security guards pushed him back...and they took you away. He said to tell you that your security guard was too aggressive and too mean.

Ali: Will he be back tomorrow?

Me: Yes, he said he'd be back.

Ali: Then make sure I see him, okay? You make sure I meet him.

Me: Okay. I really understood how he felt.

Ali: Jean...sometimes the king has a real big heart. Almost too big for his own good. And the king wants to make everybody in the world happy…all the time. It's just one king and millions of people. Sometimes the king has to be protected from all of the people pulling at him. Not because the king is mean, and not because the king doesn't love the people. But because it's just one king. Sometimes the king's soldiers have to be harsh…for the king's sake.

Me: Oh Muhammad, that is so sweet.

If anybody can do it, you can do it. But I'm not gonna sugarcoat this for you.

Conversation 8

Me: (On the phone) I need your opinion on something.

Ali: What is it?

Me: What do you think about me becoming a boxing promoter?

Ali: A BOXING PROMOTER?! Are you serious?!

Me: Yes, what do you think?

Ali: If anybody can do it, you can do it. But I'm not gonna sugarcoat this for you. Being a boxing promoter is at least 10 times harder than being a boxing manager.

Me: Really?

Ali: Because everything is on you. You have to deal with at least 10 boxers on each card. The venue. The security guards. The tickets. Everything is on you. And you have to pay everybody.

Me: Oh…Muhammad, it sounds so hard.

Ali: That's because it is so hard. And not to mention injuries. If any boxer on the card is injured while running…or in the gym, you have to replace that boxer. You have to get bonded. You have to put up money. There are just so many things to deal with.

Me: If I could push a button and your company still did promoting, I would. Then I wouldn't have to become a promoter.

Ali: Why do you want all of that on you? And it's gonna be even harder for you because you're a woman. You already know that. Look what you went through as a manager.

Me: Muhammad, I didn't just wake up this morning and say, "Wow, I have nothing better to do today. Oh golly gee, I think I'll become a boxing promoter." Marty needs me to become his promoter.

Ali: There are a lot of promoters out there. I know they would promote Marty. A world-class heavyweight boxer…number 4 in the world.

Me: Though *you* know, I've kept it a secret that Marty had back surgery. He's been out of the ring since the Page fight. It broke my heart to see Marty in the ring before the Page fight needing back surgery; and people watching him on TV didn't know what was wrong with him. I want to bring him back a certain way.

Ali: How many boxers' wives say…I don't like the way things are going…so I'll just become a boxing promoter for my husband?

Me: Wait…wait…Muhammad, I have called Don King, Butch Lewis, The Goosens, and every other promoter I know trying to get the right fight for Marty but…

Ali: Every promoter you named would promote a fight for Marty Monroe.

Me: You're right. All of them said they would but they all want him to fight somebody in the top ten. I'm not bringing Marty back like that. I know how I want to bring him back.

Ali: I don't know one boxer with the luxury of his *wife* bringing him back the way she wants to. (Laughing) I've never heard of anything like that!

Me: I've never heard of anything like that either. But that's my husband, Muhammad, and I have to be at peace with what he does in the ring. He put his career in my hands...and I don't really see that I have any other choice right now.

Ali: What does Marty think?

Me: It was *his* idea! He heard me on the phone trying to convince Don King to give me an opponent who was not in the top ten and he said, "Hang up the phone right now. And let the next call you make—be how to become a boxing promoter. You're smart. If they can do it— you can do it. From this moment on *you* are my promoter!"

Ali: (Laughing) You know Marty thinks you can fly without any wings!

Me: And Muhammad, I already asked Jimmy Lennon if he would be my announcer.

Ali: JIMMY LENNON? That means you already see yourself as a promoter. If you can see it...you can be it.

Me: (Laughing) Muhammad, I see myself in the ring with Marty and I hear Jimmy Lennon introducing me as the boxing promoter!

Ali: (Sounding like an announcer) JEEEEAN DAAAANCEEEE...
BOXING PROMOTER! If you can see it, I can see it.

Me: Can you really, Muhammad? Can you? I'm about to cry.

Ali: I can see what you want me to see. Why the tears?

Me: Because I'm grateful, soooo grateful...for being able to call
you about this.

Ali: (Playfully) Jean...there's no time for tears. You're about to make
boxing history! The *only* woman who ever managed her husband
AND promoted him!

Me: (Laughing now) HISTORY?! I'm not trying to make history.
I'm just trying to help Marty. Muhammad, you always see the best
in me. You always lift me...always.

Ali: Call me back...and let me know how it's going. And if you need
me to help you on anything...let me know.

**That same year, I became a Boxing Promoter with the legendary
Jimmy Lennon as my announcer. I promoted my first event at the
Hyatt Regency Hotel, in Downtown, Los Angeles.*

Muhammad Ali

Muhammad Ali's name is synonymous with boxing, courage, and charisma. However, the essence of Ali cannot be captured any more than we can capture the wind and put it in a bottle—or take the ocean home with us.

Muhammad Ali's name will echo in the universe until the end of time; and his memory will live on forever…in our hearts.

About The Author

Muhammad Ali fascinated a little girl with his fancy footwork in the ring and caused her to fall in love with the sport of boxing. Her biggest dream was to meet Ali. Though destiny had something even better in mind. That little girl was Jean Dancy.

Author of the poem "My Black King," the Alabama A&M University graduate is grateful to have worked as an Actress, Model, Make-up Artist, Jazz Singer, English Teacher, Sportswriter, Motivational Speaker, Life Skills Teacher, Real Estate Broker, and Certified Mediator.

However, her most outstanding accomplishment happened when she made boxing history by becoming the only woman to become both a Boxing Manager and a Boxing Promoter. Additionally, Jean is the first female to manage and later promote an athlete who was also her husband. Under Dancy's management, Marty Monroe soared to a #4 world ranking in the Heavyweight boxing division.

Dancy is also the author of "Love Guide for Teens." The popular book with teens points out how to recognize and prevent abuse in relationships.

Throughout her career, Dancy has received recognition for her achievements. Some of those achievements include being named "Woman of the Year" in sports for her accomplishments in the boxing business and being honored for becoming a member of the multi-million dollar circle of salespeople as a Real Estate Broker.

What about Muhammad Ali?—and destiny?

Jean didn't just meet Ali, she became the only female boxing manager in his Deer Lake Training Camp!

As a Sportswriter, and boxing enthusiast, Dancy has connected with some of the most elite boxers, trainers, and promoters in the history of the sport. That list includes Muhammad Ali, Joe Frazier, George Foreman, Don King, Evander Holyfield, Thomas "Hit Man" Hearns, the Mayweathers, and many more.

Jean Dancy, the mother of a lovely daughter named Ava, particularly enjoys helping people in relationships, motivational speaking, singing, and painting.

Special Thank You To:

HOLLYWOOD BASKETS

818-972-2179

www.hollywoodswagbag.com

www.hollywoodbaskets.com

www.ingramcontent.com/pod-product-compliance
Lightning Source LLC
Chambersburg PA
CBHW021824090426